Futures
that Work

USING SEARCH CONFERENCES

TO REVITALIZE COMPANIES,

COMMUNITIES AND ORGANIZATIONS

FUTURES THAT WORK

*Using Search Conferences to
Revitalize Companies, Communities
and Organizations*

**Robert Rehm
Nancy Cebula
Fran Ryan
Martin Large**

Hawthorn Press

Published by Hawthorn Press, © Copyright 2002
Hawthorn House, 1 Lansdown Lane, Stroud, Gloucestershire, GL5 1BJ. UK
Tel. (01453) 757040   Fax. (01453) 751138
E-mail: info@hawthornpress.com   Website: **www.hawthornpress.com**

Futures that Work is published by Hawthorn Press in Britain and the rest of the world, excluding North America where it is published by New Society Publishers, Gabriola Island, B.C., Canada. **www.newsociety.com** It is a co-publication by Hawthorn Press and New Society Publishers.

Cover design by Diane McIntosh
Illustrations by Abigail Large
Typeset at Hawthorn Press by Lynda Smith
Printed in the UK by The Bath Press, Bath

A catalogue record of this book is available from the British Library Cataloguing in Publication Data

ISBN 1 903458 24 2

Contents

Acknowledgements

We would like to thank the leaders, managers, and consultants whose stories enriched this book: Kader Asmal, Graham Benjamin, Catherine Bradshaw, Evangeline Caridas, Louisa Dossi, Aurilee Ferguson, Walt Grady, Paula Hartig, Frank Heckman, Sue Higgins, Steve Hobbs, Nancy Intermill, Dale Johnson, Beth Macy, Paul Mack, Beth Madison, Katheryn Martin, Dennis Mayhew, Mandla Mchunu, Terry Noseworthy, Pete Peschang, Kevin Purcell, Joan Roberts, Roy Romer, Dave Thomas, and Rich vander Broek.

Foreword

by Tom Devane

I have been studying the art and science of planning for a long
time now, with particular focus on how well plans get translated
into action after the planning process has concluded. Recently
I have noticed that what used to work well 15 years ago is no
longer effective today. Why? Because times have changed
dramatically since then. Specifically, 15 years ago:

♦ the world wasn't changing as fast as it is today. The pace of
   technological and social change now far outstrips the pace
   of changes then;

♦ it was possible for one individual, or a handful of
   individuals, to plan for an entire organization or
   community. Now the complexity in satisfying multiple
   stakeholders and balancing available resources is just too
   overwhelming for any one individual, or small group of
   people to manage well;

♦ it was possible to predict over a short period of time – say
   three to five years – what might happen in a particular
   industry or community, and design a strategic plan or
   community plan with that in mind. The luxury of prediction
   no longer exists, even for three- to five-year time spans.
   Organizations must seek to adapt quickly, and wherever
   possible exert an influence on their external environment, if
   they are to survive and thrive.

In *Futures That Work* Robert Rehm, Nancy Cebula, Fran Ryan, and Martin Large present a new way to conduct planning that is extremely relevant for the complex planning challenges facing organizations and communities today. This book is a culmination of their years of research and experience with the method, and of the experiences of those who contributed stories to the book.

This is an extremely important book for three reasons. First of all it provides a down to earth presentation of the concepts and principles of a powerful, high-leverage planning approach called a search conference. In crisp, easy-to-follow narrative and diagrams the book sets out precisely what a search conference is and the underlying principles that readers can use to design their own successful search conferences.

Second, it provides real life examples of situations where search conferences have been used and their results. Any leader – formal, or informal – considering using a high-leverage, radically different planning approach such as a search conference should critically examine case histories of where it has been used and under what conditions it succeeded. Only then can leaders decide if the new approach is appropriate for their own particular situation. This book provides them with an abundance of information necessary to determine this.

Finally, this book is important because it provides practical tips on how to plan well, whether for a corporation, community, government agency, or non-profit organization. Good planning is good planning irrespective of venue. This time-tested approach capitalizes on the tremendous power of the human spirit to create innovative plans when the right people are:

♦ assembled in a setting that fosters collaboration,
♦ charged with the responsibility of creating a desirable future that will work, and
♦ asking the right questions of themselves.

Obstacles to Developing and Executing Good Plans

A planning crisis of global proportions exists today. Though strongly worded, I do not believe this to be an overstatement. This crisis appears in businesses, government organizations, communities, and non-profit organizations. All four of these groups face five planning-related challenges: the dizzying pace of change; globalization; the collapsing of boundaries due to technology; social changes; and demanding external customers and stakeholders. There are also daunting planning challenges unique to each, as outlined below.

Businesses face five conditions that pose challenges to developing and executing good plans. These are:

- ◆ waning worker enthusiasm and intrinsic motivation;
- ◆ rewriting of the implicit employer-employee contract – specifically, employers can no longer promise lifetime employment, and workers are now demanding more development and satisfaction in their current positions;
- ◆ thinking and planning along traditional functional lines, even though much of the best work in corporations is done across departments via cross-functional teams;
- ◆ less time available for innovation and continuous improvement than ever before, because of 'lean organizations'.

In business the inability to implement a strategic plan has been the downfall of many a senior manager. A 1999 *Fortune* magazine article entitled 'Why CEOs Fail' notes that this one variable – the inability to get a strategy *executed* – was the determining factor in 70% of recent firings of CEOs, such as IBM's John Akers, Compaq's Eckard Pfeiffer, AT&T's Bob Allen, and General Motors' Robert Stempel. It wasn't the lack of a sound strategy that ousted these corporate titans – but rather lack of execution. In business there is ample cause to look for a better way of planning and executing plans. Search conferences can provide that.

Communities have their own set of planning and implementation challenges, which are different from businesses:

♦ communities are faced with rapidly shrinking funding, making it difficult to plan far ahead into the future with any certainty;
♦ community members are highly diverse, resulting in increasing difficulties in trying to satisfy members with distinctly different values and needs;
♦ multiple stakeholders with conflicting demands provide formidable challenges for communities that attempt to simultaneously address the needs of various government agencies, other regulatory bodies, and their members;
♦ corporate downsizings and 'leaner organization designs' are forcing those who have jobs to be at work longer, resulting in these people becoming less available for community work.

Clearly communities would benefit from a process that makes a diverse planning group productive quickly, creating alignment of resources and enthusiasm for implementing it. Search conferences are a natural fit for community planning.

Government organizations and non-profits share some similar challenges for developing and executing good plans. They both face:

♦ a shrinking pool of available funds that makes it difficult to take time for planning, disseminating the plan, and implementing the plan;
♦ the challenge of meeting the demands of multiple stakeholder groups with often quite different, strongly held beliefs and demands;
♦ the challenge of increasing public scrutiny.

In addition, government organizations face two unique challenges:

◆ the potential for having their world turned completely upside-down at the end of every election term, which can render planning beyond the end of the next term meaningless;
◆ government organizations that have been privatized face the demanding challenge of quickly adapting to a new set of rules necessary to compete in a business-driven, rather than government-driven environment.

Search conferences are an effective and efficient planning method that can enable organizations to deal with such problems as funding decreases, multiple stakeholder demands, and rapid environmental changes.

Traditional planning methods are missing something

Doubt about existing planning methods first began to creep into my consulting consciousness in 1995. I admit it wasn't easy to let go of the traditional practices that had served me so well over 15 years of promoting these methods and working with them in the Big Six consulting arena. The need to critically examine strengths, weaknesses, opportunities and threats (the traditional 'SWOT analysis') seemed so logical – so unswervingly right. Detailed analyses of a company's market position relative to its competitors just *had* to be the prudent thing to do. And how could an organization go wrong if they focused on their core competencies and 'stuck to the knitting'?

But history is a powerful teacher, at least to anyone paying attention. After years of working with both search conferences and traditional planning approaches, I gradually uncovered five major problems with traditional approaches.

1. They tend to extrapolate from the past rather than try to create a new future.
2. They tend to narrowly focus most attention on the company or industry situation, instead of on larger social and global trends and patterns.

3. They do little, if anything to ignite the passions of people in the organization who must implement the plan.
4. They focus on solving current problems instead of focusing on emerging patterns and on how the organization needs to change and grow.
5. Most often they address external factors individually, rather than seeking converging trends and seemingly innocuous – but often tremendously important – patterns of interrelated factors.

Benefits of search conferences

The search conference approach to planning addresses each of the above traditional planning problems and raises the stakes in strategic corporate, government, non-profit, and community planning. Benefits of a search conference come as much from the process as the product of the planning activity. Search conferences particularly excel at:

♦ focusing on the common ground of multiple stakeholders, then seeking to expand it and develop actions to implement a shared desirable future;
♦ enabling a group of people to think together;
♦ detecting and capitalizing on previously unrecognized useful patterns and trends;
♦ developing strategic thinkers and leaders at multiple levels of the organization;
♦ generating energy for implementing the strategy.

Taking that first step toward better planning

My personal experience is that leaders charged with such responsibility are interested in the answers to three key questions:

♦ What is this approach?
♦ Who has done this before, and what happened?
♦ What can be done to make this successful in my situation?

In this book the authors address each of the above pragmatic questions, helping leaders take the important first step toward better planning. In the first chapter they provide an overview of search conferences and use mini-cases to illustrate benefits and make important design points. Chapters 7 through 13 contain a wealth of diverse case histories from across the globe as told by 'people in the front line'. These case histories – approximately one half of the book – give detailed examples of what happened in search conferences held for a variety of purposes including strategic corporate planning, community planning, and planning for a youth organization in a war-ravaged territory. With both feet firmly planted on pragmatic ground, the authors inject just the right dose of theory among practical principles to help the reader design a successful search conference in chapter 4. For those interested in the nuts and bolts of conducting a search conference there is a practical step-by-step guide in chapter 2.

For those seeking better planning results, *Futures That Work* helps shape thought processes as well as planning processes. Its contribution lies not merely in highlighting search conferences as a better planning approach, but also in stimulating a better way of thinking about how we can actually influence the future and adapt quickly to changes in the external environment. This book is a treasure trove of practical experiences and easy-to-grasp principles for planning success. The authors have a solid grasp of the theory of search conferences, why they work, and how to design them for success. I highly recommend this book to anyone seeking higher levels of effectiveness, efficiency and innovation in their planning processes.

Tom Devane
April, 2002

Consultant, author with Peggy Holman, of *The Change Handbook: Group Methods for Shaping the Future.*

Introduction

Imagine bringing a group of people together for a couple of days to create the future for their community or organization. Along the way they become a community of planners who dream large about their future and create a comprehensive plan of action to make their desired future come true. Then picture people in this newly-formed community working together to carry out their plan.

That's what a search conference can do for you. It gives you a plan for the future and a community of people ready to make it happen – a future that works!

The people in a search conference could be citizens, community leaders, public officials, managers, activists, or workers in a manufacturing plant. The task they work on could range from a strategic plan for a company to changes in a city's social services. It might be a merger, the creation of a new business, improved health care in a region, economic development for an urban area, a plan to improve productivity in a factory, or a plan to protect the environment.

Futures That Work is all about search conferences: what happens in them and what results you can expect from doing them. The book describes underlying principles of a search conference and how these principles come to life before your eyes. It gives practical advice on how to plan a search conference and how to sustain changes that come about as a result. And it is packed with examples of actual search conferences that made change happen in a variety of systems.

The search conference did not just pop up overnight; it's not one of those management fads. Search conferencing has a long, rich history. The first search conference happened in 1960 in Great Britain, when leaders of two aircraft engine manufacturers came together to merge their two companies into one. The inventors of the method and the leaders of that first search were social scientists Fred Emery and Eric Trist.

Since 1960, search conferences have occurred around the world on a range of topics and in a wide variety of forms. Eric Trist spread the word about search to many parts of the world, spawning a creative flow of designs and styles. Fred and Merrelyn Emery developed their own way of search conferencing in Australia, planting the seed in North America and the rest of the globe. Other search conference variations have been developed around the world as well.

Fred and Merrelyn Emery influenced us the most. We are grateful to them for teaching us their way of searching. The four of us have evolved our own variations on search conferencing over the years. This book is the product of our experience doing search conferences in different parts of the world with a wide variety of community and organizational systems. We hope that you will develop your own ways of searching just as we did.

We wrote the book for any community leader, activist or citizen wanting to learn a creative and energizing way to plan for the future of their community, on issues such as environment, health, social services or education. The search conference is a community-building approach that produces new relationships and real action. The book is also ideal for leaders of corporate or public sector organizations interested in producing strategic plans to make their organizations or departments more effective and adaptable in our fast-changing environment. And we think this book will give human resources professionals a useful tool for bringing people together to make effective, creative change happen for their organization and the people who work in it.

Search conferencing has gained broad acceptance over the decades. We think the time is now right for searching to take off and become a more widespread means of change in communities and workplaces. Fred Emery and Eric Trist, the creators of the search conference, coined the term "turbulent environment" to describe the way global change is accelerating these days. Our fast-changing environment has brought many benefits – instant communications, medical breakthroughs, and a host of technological innovations. But there is also a troubling downside.

Change is happening so fast today that people in organizations cannot keep up. Emery and Trist thought that unless people got a grip on their increasingly turbulent environments, they would soon feel more and more alienated from their society: instead of experiencing one another as important to their own future, they would withdraw into isolated private worlds, trying to cope with the uncertainty of a turbulent world by being indifferent to it or cynical toward institutions such as government, big business, and the media. This, Emery and Trist believed, would lead to over-simplification of big contemporary problems, which people would come to perceive in black-and-white terms as issues of right versus wrong, good versus evil. At the same time they would shrink from taking responsibility for solving problems in their communities and workplaces.

We think this is an accurate description of what is happening too often in today's world – not always, not everywhere, but enough to cause concern. The antidote is active participation – individuals working together to create action-focused communities based on shared ideals about their system's future.

So we see the search conference as a practical way to build communities of people who go out to meet the challenges of our unpredictable times and take responsibility for making change happen in a purposeful way. As the world becomes more and more turbulent, the need is great for people to create communities to search for their desirable futures together. The search conference puts people in the driver's seat of change, so they can steer together toward the future they want for their system, making adjustments as they go forward.

Part One of *Futures That Work* is all about the search conference. It features the principles, a step-by-step design, and examples needed to understand the method's power, plus useful information on how to prepare and follow up a search conference.

Chapter 1, "Search Conference", takes you right inside the room where a search conference is underway and describes what is going on. Then the chapter shifts to an array of real search conference stories – brief vignettes that showcase the variety of search conference applications from public to private sectors, from community to corporate settings.

In chapter 2, "Search Conference Design – The Open Systems Funnel", we walk you step-by-step through the basic search conference design to give you an accurate picture of what to expect when you do a conference. This includes the three search conference phases – learning about the environment, learning about the system, and action-planning. Following the description of a typical search conference comes the story, in chapter 3, of the Nebraska Mental Health search conference. This compelling, system-changing story brings to life each step of the search conference design, showing the power of the method for producing significant change right here and now.

Chapter 4 discusses the various principles and concepts underlying every search conference. *Open systems theory* shows how any system – whether community or corporation – can learn from and affect its external environment. *Ecological learning* guides the down-to-earth, learning-by-doing way of searching. Using what we call the *democratic design principle* assures that search conference participants take control of their own planning. Every search conference sets up conditions in which *democratic dialogue* can take place. Conflict management happens through the discovery of common ground agreement among participants. And *group dynamics* principles keep the group focused on its agreed task.

Preparation is the key for any search conference to be successful and produce lasting change, so most of the conditions for doing successful searches revolve around effective preparation. Chapter 5 goes into detail on every planning issue, including setting up a planning group for the search, identifying the conference task and purpose, and selecting participants. The chapter ends with a discussion of logistical concerns – where to have the conference, how much time the conference will take, how many people, and conference room arrangements.

Chapter 6 is about follow-up after the search conference ends, describing how you can use a participative design workshop to organize implementation groups so that they are clear on their task and process. Chapter 7 describes critical mass theory and its application to search conferencing as a way of spreading and sustaining the innovations coming out of the search. We return to the Nebraska mental health story discussed earlier in the book, and spell out how the changes decided at that first conference spread through the state of Nebraska over the past several years.

Part Two of the book is a collection of search conference stories covering a variety of systems – corporate, community, and public sector. The storytellers are the people who were involved in the design and facilitation of each conference.

Frank Heckman, in chapter 8, takes us inside the search conference that developed the Macatawa, Michigan regional plan and shows how citizens and leaders carried out important action plans together. In chapter 9 Kevin Purcell and Robert Rehm tell the story of how a Microsoft products group used a search conference for product planning, and how the constructive use of conflict led them to a creative solution nobody expected.

Chapter 10 is about how water engineers, at the behest of the Governor of Colorado, used a search conference to produce a regional water plan that would prevent the building of a dam. Nancy Cebula and Evangeline Caridas bring us the story in chapter 11 of a small benefits company that did a search conference with all its employees to discover ways to manage rapid growth, and in the process also found ways to integrate the achievement and relationship sides of their business. They called it the "Hoop and the Tree".

Chapter 12 stretches the boundaries of search conferencing. In it Graham Benjamin shows how a big energy company applied search conference principles and concepts to create stakeholder alignment in a major building project. In Chapter 13 Steve Hobbs relates the amazing story of the YMCA in Palestine doing search conferences to discover their desirable future in an environment of political upheaval.

We start with a description of what happens in a search conference.

Part One:

All About
Search Conferences

Chapter 1

What Happens in a Search Conference?

A search conference is a participative planning event that enables people to create a plan for the most desirable future of their community or organization, a plan they carry out themselves.

You can use a search conference to create change in a city, state, region, or at a national level in relation to any issue of concern to people, such as the environment, education, health, or economic development. Or you can use it for strategic planning for a company or public sector organization, or any department or division of a larger organization.

People have used search conferences for new companies just starting up, for two organizations merging, and when several organizations want to integrate their service delivery. Search conferences have also helped industries and associations plan their future development.

In this chapter we give you an overview of what it is like to be in a search conference, and provide you with a number of quick vignettes of search conferences that have taken place in recent years.

A search conference is about learning, change and community building. No matter what the topic or system, every search conference produces these outcomes:

♦ A comprehensive plan for the future of a system. The plan spells out the changes people in the conference agree to make to improve the system. It includes the system's new purpose, goals, and action steps to get change underway. And the plan shows how the changed system is adaptive in its turbulent environment.

♦ A community of people with the energy and desire to carry out the plan they have made together. People leave the conference with the enthusiasm and commitment required to spread their learning to others back home.

♦ People who have learned about their fast-changing environment and have the tools to keep on searching in the future. They have developed the capacities they need to continue fine-tuning and changing their plan as they implement it.

The Search Conference Experience

When you enter the room to begin a search conference you join 20 to 40, or maybe more, people who are there because they are an important part of their system. They will be managers and organization leaders if the search conference task is to create a new strategic plan for an organization. Or, if it is a community search conference, participants will be community leaders, public officials, and citizens with knowledge and interest in the issue being searched, such as the community's economic future or improving social services. You and your fellow participants have been invited to the search conference not to represent the interests of others who don't attend, but because you are important to the conference task and purpose.

As you look around at all the people in the room, imagine the group as a human jigsaw puzzle. In the next couple of days you will focus on putting the puzzle pieces of strategy together that will produce your system's most desirable future. In the room, each person contributes knowledge about some piece of the overall puzzle. The idea is to get the right people, such as you, in the room: those whose participation is critical for doing the job of planning for the future.

When we use the word "participative" in the search conference, this takes the word further than its usual meaning. A search conference is not about a group giving input to higher-up people in authority who are responsible for planning. Participation in a search means the group actually creates and carries out its own plan. That's why it is important to keep the number of participants at a level where face-to-face community can emerge.

The search conference is not the usual visioning process that has been so trendy over recent years. We frequently encounter organizations and communities that have produced creative, abstract vision statements that are framed on the wall and get them nowhere. The search conference rivets people's attention on real action based on a future the group wants to make happen.

The conference normally lasts three days, preferably off-site and overnight. You and other participants immerse yourselves in a "social island" setting in which you will form new relationships and commitments. During the conference people work together as a large conference community, with small groups for specific tasks.

We call it "searching" because the conference community searches through its external environment and system, collecting, analyzing, and synthesizing data. The reason for searching through your system's turbulent environment is that for your system to thrive in the world, it has to be adaptive within its environment. Your system has to find ways to plan actively, so that your system is both responding to and changing its environment as it goes. We call it "active adaptation."

Adapting does not just mean getting faster or being more flexible or accommodating. It means actively developing your system's capacity to continuously learn from and change its environment. Your system can *reduce* turbulence by changing the conditions that surround it and by influencing its future direction.

The search conference is designed to provide a learning environment in which participation is equal and open, regardless of hierarchy or position. People's words are recorded on chart paper for all to see. There are no individual workbooks, as the emphasis is on restoring oral culture, dialogue, and discussion.

You will notice that the search conference has no lectures, speeches, keynote addresses, or training sessions. There is nothing to make it appear that people are in a training workshop or traditional conference in which expertise resides in the presenters. And there is no need for people to experience chaos for learning or change to occur. You will experience nothing mysterious in a search conference – just people doing real work on important tasks.

Professional facilitators lead the search conference. They have the training to do the job and are experienced in conference design, leadership, and use of search principles. You can expect these facilitators to be responsible for providing clear, appropriate tasks for the group to do and they manage time for you in a way that allows deliberation and true dialogue to occur. What you will *not* see facilitators do is participate in the content of your discussions. That's your job, not theirs.

Towards the middle of the search conference, after you have discussed and analyzed what's been happening in your system and its environment, you work in small groups to create your system's most desirable future. You share your ideas of how to make your system better than ever. And together as a conference community, you agree on which future ideas to make happen.

You spend most of the third day of the search conference setting up plans of action to bring your desirable future down to earth to make sure it really comes true. As you leave the search conference, you know what you and the others are going to do next in specific terms, in the next weeks and months, to implement your plan. You leave feeling satisfied, with a sense of inner joy about what you have accomplished together.

Stories from Search Conferences

Below are glimpses into several actual search conferences. These stories cover a wide array of search conference applications from corporate to public sector, from small business to big, from strategic planning to process improvement, and include important community issues such as crime and social services. Reading these short search stories gives you an idea of the variety of uses for a search conference.

Strategic planning at Hewlett Packard
by Robert Rehm

The Hewlett Packard search conference occurred in a major manufacturing plant employing about 2,200 people. A new general manager had just been assigned to the plant. His task was to renew a business that had suffered from some difficult business changes. The GM knew about the search conference from his previous position and quickly decided to use the method to bring key plant managers together around new directions and plans to re-energize the business. He invited the plant site's leading manufacturing, engineering, and marketing managers, as well as some of the more "informal" leaders from the workforce. There was no lengthy preparation and no planning group. There was no time to waste for the GM to get things started. Most of the managers of the plant were meeting the new GM for the first time at the search conference.

The purpose of the search conference was straightforward: to develop a plan for renewing the business top to bottom. Participants were pre-briefed before the conference and knew what to expect when they arrived. There was a lot on the line for everyone and the task was complex and compelling.

The search conference was scheduled for four days because of the broad scope and complexity of the event. The first session began after dinner on a Monday night and the last session ended at 2 p.m. on Thursday. In between, people worked a feverish twelve hours on both Tuesday and Wednesday. The excitement and tension was high.

It did not take long for common ground to develop, as well as some important differences. It became clear early on that there was significant tension over the direction the plant should take: which key products to keep making and which to drop. The tension over product direction reached a peak during the strategy and action-planning phase when people demanded that a firm decision be made about which products to stop making. The large group authorized a small sub-group to go out of the room and make the decision, a decision everyone agreed to respect. This decision was critical as it affected the basic business direction of the plant.

The result of this important search conference was commitment to a thorough strategic plan that people agreed to carry out and support back at the plant. The new general manager walked away from the search conference with a comprehensive strategic plan to renew an important division of the company. He smiled because he realized the conference had built a community of leaders ready to take action. He was off to a good start with his new assignment.

Transforming the South African Department of Water Affairs and Forestry
by Steve Hobbs, Mandla Mchunu, and Robert Rehm

In 1995, South Africa's Department of Water Affairs and Forestry (DWAF) commissioned an institutional transformation process to increase the department delivery's efficiency, and make it more people-oriented and democratic. The search conference was used as the transformational tool in this process. Kader Asmal, Minister of Water Affairs and Forestry, rejected what he called a "forcible" transformation process in favor of a participative approach to change. He reasoned that as all South Africa was transforming to democracy, so important governmental institutions like DWAF should also use a democratic process for change.

The driving force for change was the vision of the new government that it needed to transform all its institutions to heal the country from its apartheid past, becoming a society based on equity and justice. According to Kader Asmal, when the newly elected government of President Nelson Mandela came into power in 1994, "14,000 villages with between 12 and 15 million people did not have access to clean water, and around 21 million had no hygienic sanitation." During the apartheid era, the department focused its energy on engineering and large dam building, serving the needs mostly of the privileged white population.

DWAF did a series of ten search conferences, one in each of the country's nine provinces and the tenth for the head office. Participants included managers and workers from all levels and areas of the organization. External stakeholders also participated. They included people from the agriculture industry, local government, NGOs, trade unions, consumer groups, environmentalists, private companies, as well as people who were not being serviced.

The process culminated in a national transformational conference designed to integrate strategies coming out of the provinces. At this national conference, representatives from the provincial search conferences gathered to share the work they had done. Then they came up with an overarching vision, strategies, and a new slogan: "Ensuring Some For All Forever!" After the national conference, people returned to their provinces to communicate the new vision and strategies. Then people from the original provincial conferences worked to create specific action plans for their province. The whole process took ten months.

The transformation process launched strategies in several areas. One result was a new water catchment management system. Including external stakeholders in the transformation process made it possible to develop strategies that brought water users and others directly into the running of DWAF. Now water users and department representatives sit on catchment management authorities that make important decisions about water resources.

Many participants credited the transformation process with improving relationships and communication across race, management, and external stakeholder boundaries. They appreciated the open, transparent interaction they experienced in the search conferences, and claimed that was a major part of the transformation.

In a transformation progress report in 1999, Kader Asmal reported that millions of people previously un-served because of race now had clean water and hygienic sanitation. He also stated that the transformation brought into top and middle management people who had been previously excluded, such as blacks and women. The process produced a department that is now efficient and effective, responsive to the needs of the community, and representative of the new South Africa.

Juvenile summit in suburban Denver
by Robert Rehm

Several years ago, the Denver metropolitan area was suffering from a rash of juvenile crime, especially drive-by shootings in neighborhoods and gang-related offenses in the suburbs. People were worried that a criminal epidemic was underway. The district attorney of one of the counties near Denver organized a juvenile summit to discuss the issues with concerned citizens, county agencies, schools, law enforcement, and local government. He used the search conference as the format for the summit. The meeting was scheduled over three days. Its purpose was to find creative ways to both prevent and respond to juvenile crime in the county.

Participants included the chief judge, a state senator, mayors, police officers and chiefs, high school students, juvenile offenders, teachers and school administrators, probation officials, business people, youth service agencies, and citizens at large. During the critical phase in which people work in small groups to create their system's most desirable future, one group was composed of the chief judge, a police officer, a juvenile offender just out of a Department of Corrections facility, and several others. It was amazing to see these people from such different backgrounds and experiences putting their heads together to find solutions for problems they were knowledgeable about.

The search conference resulted in a handful of practical projects and action plans. The most impressive was a proposal for a juvenile assessment center – a clearing-house where at-risk juveniles could be quickly linked to available services. It took about a year to get the building built and staffed. Within another year, the center's success rate was over 80%, a terrific result for such a program. In the program, assessment specialists can call on an entire spectrum of county resources to assist young people. Included are programs for chemical abuse, tutoring at school, suicide counseling, and a range of community services.

Etheria Day Spa: search conference turns ideas into action
by Evangeline Caridas

In 1996, Louisa Dossi wanted to follow an industry trend by transforming her successful salon, "Giovanni", into a day spa. More than a business maneuver, this was the dream Dossi shared with her husband. They worked many years for others before opening Giovanni, and growing their business into a day spa seemed "a natural expansion".

Before initiating plans and investments for growth, Dossi wanted her team on board. She hoped to preserve Giovanni's close, friendly atmosphere throughout the expansion, to continue offering her clients and employees the best possible experience, while increasing professional opportunities and services.

Dossi's solution was to do a search conference. "We'd never done anything like this!" Dossi recalls. A search conference helped Giovanni's entire staff discuss how their professional development might be affected by changes at the salon and in the industry. The experience helped the staff come together in favor of growth. "It was exciting to be going forward," Dossi says, "to invest in big projects and long-term plans, because we had a committed staff."

Giovanni planned for slow, steady growth, but there were immediate visible results. The salon grew busier, as staff found creative ways to succeed as individual workers and as part of the business. Dossi's dream soon materialized: Etheria Day Spa opened in October 2000.

Dossi credits skills learned in the search conference for creating a peaceful environment for clients and staff alike. The contentment of Etheria's staff shows in high retention and growth rates: the staff has increased by 50%, and only one employee has left. Expanding into hydrotherapy and special events, Etheria offers exciting new services to its large base of Giovanni clients. Dossi says the search conference "helped us be right where we wanted to be."

A search conference for the Austin Independent School District
by Evangeline Caridas

The Austin Independent School District's Department of Professional Development (DPD) provides training and career planning to all school employees in the greater Austin, Texas area. Administrators, support staff, teachers, and custodial staff all depend on the DPD for job placement services and support programs.

But personnel were split between two locations and multiple tasks. The stratification concerned new Director Dr. Paul Mack. Employees lacked both a vision for DPD, and a structure for effective communication. Although responding to clients' basic expectations, Dr. Mack knew the DPD could – and should – do better. Just one layer removed from schoolchildren, his team was responsible for supporting every employee of Austin's school system.

Dr. Mack wanted to bring his people together under a common vision that encouraged everyone's participation. He initiated a search conference to help people learn what others were doing, work from others' knowledge, develop a concerted mission, and create a cooperative, supportive workplace.

Dr. Mack introduced participative strategies to people accustomed to working as individuals, not as a team. Obstacles to communication were deeply entrenched, and employees were "reluctant to voice their opinions on the same level with their bosses". The strict hierarchy imposed by Dr. Mack's predecessor created widespread anxiety about job security. People kept their knowledge private, working independently and interpreting cooperative ventures as threatening interferences.

Everyone appreciated this opportunity to exhibit their individual knowledge, discuss the DPD's mission, and create an action plan. After the search conference, immediate, visible enhancements stimulated improvement of "all the intangible and unmeasurable attributes of a productive workplace". Dr. Mack brought the DPD together at one site, allowing direct contact, and helping everyone understand all that DPD did. Dr. Mack says that thanks to the search conference, "We learned to be a high-performing team that successfully supports all school employees, and helps them improve student achievement in Austin's school system."

Chapter 1
What
Happens in
a Search
Conference

Addressing social problems in a rural Alaska native village
by Pete Peschang

Significant events in the latter half of the 20th century left many Alaska native villages in a state of cultural confusion, economically unstable, and with some of the highest rates of social problems in the nation. Treatment of substance abuse, suicide, child abuse, and other social problems in rural villages has largely been misunderstood and neglected for decades and has had a devastating impact on the social and cultural fabric of the villages.

One tribe recently used a search conference to engage its tribal members in addressing their own social problems. The search was well attended and participants completed a comprehensive planning process for the village that included extensive discussions about social problems. During the shared history, the group traced the onset of social problems to the boarding school era when many youth were sent away, creating a major disruption to traditional village life. Some had good experiences but others suffered abuse. At the same time the village experienced wholesale changes to its traditional way of life, such as the introduction of alcohol and people turning away from traditional healing practices.

As the group processed the information, they gained a greater understanding of the problems, and collectively agreed that it was time for a community-wide healing process. Their action-planning outlined a broad-based plan for healing and formed a working group to refine and implement their plans. Since the conference, the working group has defined their mission, appointed a special sub-committee to address on-going social problems and submitted proposals for community education and social services. The search has united the village and helped them organize efforts to move beyond this destructive phase in their history so they can get on with their vision for the future.

The Rexdale Partners search conference
by Catherine Bradshaw and Joan Roberts

Throughout 2000, the members of Rexdale Partners were feeling increasingly burned out. This loosely structured network of community organizations and social service agencies in Northwest Metro, Toronto, had worked hard for the last 30 years to meet the needs of a community that was falling further and further behind Toronto's economic boom. The amalgamation in 1998 of the various cities in Toronto's vicinity into one "megacity" had wrested control and financial support from many of the smaller communities. This, plus government cutbacks and the demands of a global economy, had further marginalized the Rexdale community and placed increasingly complex demands on its local institutions. Rexdale Partners, mandated to advocate for the community at all levels of government, found itself losing steam and focus. The search conference offered a way to develop a common vision and strategic plan for how to work together to improve the Rexdale community.

The search conference was held in February 2001. It proved to be helpful in a number of important ways. Data came out in an excited rush during the environmental scan, as people shared their perceptions of the world beyond their community. This segment of the conference was critical in lifting people's awareness beyond their individual agencies and helping them see how they were all connected to a broader social field. Another high point was the history scan. As the "anciens" shared their memories, newer members were astonished to learn about previous successes in areas where Rexdale Partners no longer worked, and inspired by the innovation and hard work that had kept the organization alive and kicking for over thirty years.

Nearly a year after the search conference, a meeting between community leaders and the conference managers revealed that the Rexdale search conference had had a lasting impact on the community. In addition to the implementation of one main action plan, the dynamics around the table at monthly meetings have improved as a result of new relationships built during the search conference. People work more from a common picture of the needs and strengths of the community that they serve. They're more aware of their interconnectedness and are eager to provide support for each other's initiatives.

Improving the outbound travel experience at United Airlines
by Dennis Mayhew

The international airport in Denver, Colorado is one of the world's premier airports. United Airlines is its biggest passenger carrier, and a critical hub within the United Airlines system. However, a new airport does not assure a smooth operation. For an airline locked into a traditional management structure within a hierarchical organization, the search conference was a bold, new approach to planning.

The United hub at Denver was lagging behind current expectations: morale was suffering and a consistent number of employee grievances were being filed. Many on the senior team were new to their positions and the General Manager was new to the company. Corporate headquarters was pressuring the Denver hub to pay particular attention to improving the "turn times" of the airplanes connecting between other hubs and smaller airports. Delay at Denver had a negative compounding impact on the rest of the system.

The Denver General Manager decided to use the search conference as a change methodology. The search conference met the immediate critical operational needs, while coinciding with the corporate emphasis of using teams and engaging more people in planning their work. As the conference task the senior team selected: "Improving the outbound travel experience of the customer."

The senior team determined that customers encountered

United and airport personnel in four different segments throughout their "outbound experience" in moving through the airport. The four segments were lobby check-in, pre-flight, boarding, and information systems. Four redesign teams were formed, one for each segment. Each team included workers from many functions, representing each facet of the airport including ramp service, customer service, mechanics, pilots, flight attendants, vendor services, and the regional airline partner. The participants in the search conference were senior management and the four redesign teams, as well as elected employees representing union grievance committees.

Here are some examples of improvements agreed upon at the search conference by the lobby check-in team: a complete change of the lobby layout by rearranging the check-in counters that served the various customers. This resulted in vast improvements to the entire customer flow through the lobby and coincided with the curbside signage. And, working with the police and airport authorities, officers were stationed to relieve traffic bottlenecks and additional security stations were opened during daily peak times.

The conference ended with people feeling very excited and encouraged about the opportunities before them. Following the conference, each redesign team worked full-time for a number of months in the further development of its ideas. The enthusiasm generated by this work created the impetus for a complete work redesign at this hub, centering on team-based organizational concepts, where work decisions were pushed down to the lowest level of the hierarchy.

Summary

In this chapter, we have provided you with a brief, high-level view into the search conference, including stories from conferences that have been done on a variety of topics for a diverse range of systems. Now it is time to dig in deeper and learn about the basic design of a typical search conference.

Chapter 2

Search Conference Design – The Open Systems Funnel

This chapter describes in detail the basic design of a typical search conference. You can tailor this model to fit the needs of your system, so your search conference will be unique. It is not an off-the-shelf design, not one size fits all.

Seeing this basic design gives you a complete picture of what to expect from doing a search conference. The story of the Nebraska mental health search conference follows in Chapter 3 to bring this design to life. It shows how one system applied and adapted this basic design. Then Chapter 4 covers all the principles and concepts that make search conferencing a dynamic process.

The design of a search conference is an application of open systems theory. This is a concept that says that any system – whether an organization or community – has an open and direct relationship with its larger environment. A system learns from its environment and, in turn, changes its environment in a purposeful way.

The search conference resembles a funnel in its design. It begins with the widest possible perspective, outside you and your system. Then it narrows to specific key strategies and actions, widening again as the group implements its plan back home and spreads its learning to other people who were not in the room. Here is the basic design:

Changes in the world important to your system's future

Your system's history: appreciating where
your system came from

Your current system: what to
keep, drop, and create

Most desirable
system

Strategies and
action plans

Community implements its plan
and spreads its learning to other people back home

In a nutshell, the pattern of a search conference runs as follows:

♦ It begins with people learning about their turbulent,
  uncertain global environment
♦ Next, the group searches through its system's past and
  present in order to create the most desirable system.
♦ Then people develop strategies and action plans that they
  will implement.

Roughly one third of the conference time focuses on *learning about the turbulent environment*, one third on *learning about the system*, and the last third concentrates on *action-planning*.

A search conference usually begins in the late afternoon or early evening. All the participants have attended pre-briefing meetings beforehand, so everyone knows what to expect. The conference opens with a welcome from the sponsor of the event and a short statement of the conference task and its importance to the future of the system that is the subject of the search.

Next, the conference facilitators review the agenda and design, and ask people to form small groups to discuss their expectations and hopes for the search conference. Once the groups' expectations are presented and clarified, the search conference is underway. There are no icebreakers, speeches, or any activities that suggest that this is one of those traditional conferences in which someone besides the participants does the work.

21

Chapter 2
Search
Conference
Design – the
Open Systems
Funnel

Learning about the Environment

In this first part, people share their impressions of what has been happening in the world over the last several years that is important for them to consider as they plan for the future. We call this part "changes in the world important to your system's future".

People voice their perceptions aloud in the large group setting. The ground rule is simple: all perceptions of the environment are valid and are written on chart paper for all to see.

The changing world appears before everyone's eyes as the list grows. Examples are:

♦ movement toward a global economy
♦ intensifying environmental problems
♦ expanding global communication and technology
♦ increasing government regulation
♦ more empowerment in workplaces.

The list goes on and on, covering many sheets of chart paper. And all the charts go up on the wall, and stay up there for the entire conference so everything is public and above board.

A lot happens at once. People see that their organization or community exists within a much larger context, and they start to take responsibility for their own data. They act in an open and public manner, beginning to build a planning community of trust. Doing this session as a total community sends the message that the search conference is a community-building event.

Next, small task groups form to make sense of their data. Sense-making is an important part of any search conference. It is how a group discovers its common ground. The small groups discuss and agree upon such issues as:

♦ the impact of global changes on our system
♦ what the future of the global environment will likely be, or
♦ what kind of world we desire.

The small groups present their findings to one another to see their commonalities and differences. And again, the chart paper goes up on the wall and stays there for the duration of the search.

The reason for starting with the environment is that there is a direct connection between the future direction of any organization or community and the direction of the larger global environment. It's the system and environment acting on one another that determine any new state of affairs. When system and environment are moving in sync, they are co-creating the future together.

In corporate and public sector organizational searches, another level of the environment needs to be scanned and understood. This is the organization's direct business or task environment – those changes just outside the boundary of the system that are having the most immediate effect on the future of the organization. Examples from corporate searches include industry trends, technological innovations, customer expectations, competitors' strategies, government regulations, and changes in the parent company or organization if the system is part of a larger entity.

Here's a diagram illustrating open systems theory, showing the task/business environment as that part of the environment closest to the system. The diagram indicates that people in a search learn from the environment – the changing world and the task/business environments – and develop a plan for the future that they take out into the world.

23

Chapter 2
Search
Conference
Design – the
Open Systems
Funnel

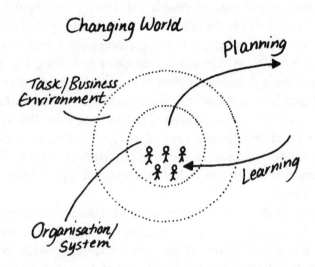

At this point in a search conference, this diagram is presented (see chapter 4 for a further explanation of this diagram). The task is to identify in the large group things that are changing in the business/task environment. Then small groups take a closer look at the items from the list and pinpoint those items that will have the most impact on the system and their future implications. Each group reports back to the larger search community so all can hear the results of the analyses. Then the group looks for common ground agreement and notes the differing points of view. This list can be referred back to during the strategy and action-planning phase as these items may be constraints in the environment that need to be dealt with in order for the plans to be successful.

Learning about the System

By now it may be mid-morning of the second day, and time to move from the environment into the system being searched. Three things happen next: people appreciate their history as a system, learn about the current functioning of the system, and then agree on their system's most desirable future.

The purpose of the <u>history</u> session is to appreciate shared perspectives of the past so people can learn from them before creating the future. In the history session, people recall important events, milestones, and turning points in the history of the system. This is important because appreciating a system's history makes it possible for people to create a future that links the past and future. As people share their viewpoints about the system's past, patterns emerge. Finding out how the system developed and becoming aware of the patterns enables people to make conscious choices about which aspects of their system they want to continue, and what to stop or change as they move into the future.

History is also important in a search conference because it plays an important role in community building. Normally, in a search, history is done as an open dialogue, with people recalling aloud their memories of events they believe shaped their system. The ground rule is this: all perceptions of the past are valid and to be respected. One person's memory of an event may be totally different from another's. It is just like the Japanese film *Rashomon*, in which several witnesses to an event have different recollections about what actually happened. It's the shared history – including the differing points of view – that make a history session so powerful and compelling. The history session restores the kind of oral culture that is essential to the community-building process.

It often works to start with the "old timers" of the system, the people who have been a part of the system for the longest time. They become educators in the search conference, giving their perspectives on how the system was formed and how it developed. By the time it is over, everyone who wants to has contributed his or her point of view. People are surprised and enlightened at what they hear in such a history. Old assumptions about the past are laid bare, as the past is revived and made present. In the history session, the search community discovers together the unique features and characteristics of the system, informing itself about what's important for the future.

History leads naturally and quickly into a discussion of the system's <u>current functioning</u>. A straightforward, yet comprehensive way to do this is to assess:

Chapter 2
Search
Conference
Design – the
Open Systems
Funnel

- ◆ what about the system to keep as it is because it is working
- ◆ what to drop or get rid of, and
- ◆ what to create about the system that doesn't exist today.

We call this "keep, drop, and create". One way to do it is to brainstorm keep, drop, and creates on chart paper. The usual ground rule applies: all perceptions are valid. And items can appear on more than one list. One person's keep can be another person's drop, and a third person's create. The create list is often a prelude to the third part of learning about the system, the most desirable future. Energy is peaking at this point and people are ready to create the future.

By this point it is most likely just after lunch on day two. People break into small mixed groups that work in parallel on the same task: the <u>most desirable future</u> of the system. By mixed groups, we mean each group has a mixture of people from various parts of the system. There are no fixed ways for groups to work. Groups manage themselves to come up with lists of specific points describing the desirable system, as it would look at an agreed time in the future – say five years out. The groups report and integrate their results. Then the entire conference community decides which points to develop into desirable strategic goals.

It is important that this session result in a whole array of desirable future points, so as not to put all the emphasis on one overarching theme. You know the old saying, "Don't put all your eggs in one basket." The group decides the number of desirable future points to select, based on what they think they can handle.

Action-planning

It is now the third and final day of the search conference. The search community spends this whole day developing their desirable future into specific strategies and action plans. They have learned about their environment and its effect on the system. They have learned about their system and created their desirable future for it. Now it is time to plan how they will take their changed system back home.

To begin with, everyone chooses the specific desirable future point he or she wants to work on. People then form small groups to develop action plans for each point. It is important that each group understand that it is working for the entire community, not just itself.

The whole conference community brainstorms and agrees on the components of the action plans so that there is some consistency across groups. The community decides how much overall time to dedicate to action-planning. Within that period, groups choose their own way of working. They are self-managing.

The components of the action-planning process typically include:

A clear statement of strategic goals. This is a matter of accurately translating the desirable future points into strategic goals that are consistent with and respect the work the whole community did earlier when it decided on its future. The goal statement should be clear enough for people to understand just by reading it.

Ways around key constraints. The best strategies are indirect. By indirect we mean that they encircle, get around, or undercut key constraints that exist, as opposed to directly confronting barriers head on. The constraints we are talking about here are the barriers to change that exist in the environment that people discussed on the first day. Putting the emphasis on ways around constraints instead of on the constraints themselves helps people discover constructive ideas that become the seeds of strategy and action.

Specific action steps. What are people going to do to reach the strategic goal? What are the specific actions that make the most sense? Concentrate especially on realistic first steps.

Timeframes. What is the overall timeline for the action plan? Include both long and short-term targets that are flexible and realistic.

Who is responsible and involved? Once the action steps are identified, it is time to determine who is going to what. Is this action-planning group going to stay together to implement its plan or are there other people more appropriate for the task? Are there people in other groups or not here at the search conference who should be invited to join in implementing the plan? How will people coordinate and control their work together?

Resources. What information, technologies, equipment, and money do people need in order to implement the plan?

Measurement. How will the groups know if and when they have accomplished the goal? What measures of success should they choose? And who will monitor the action plan and how will they do it?

Chapter 2
Search
Conference
Design – the
Open Systems
Funnel

The action-planning work is split into two or three parts, separated by interim reports from all the groups. Since the small action-planning groups are actually working on behalf of the whole community at this point, it is important to periodically do progress reports to gather feedback and suggestions. After all, the entire plan belongs to the whole community that is responsible for carrying it out. After each interim report the small groups get back to work on adjusting their plan and continuing with the steps spelled out above.

Towards the end of the day, each group makes a final report and the search conference goes into its final large group session involving the whole search community. It is at this point that people discuss next steps. It is critical to be as clear as possible about who is doing what next about action-planning.

This next steps conversation covers these issues:

♦ Who will collect the chart paper on the walls and complete a report?
♦ When will the action-planning groups meet again?
♦ How will the work of the groups be coordinated?
♦ When will the whole community meet again?
♦ How will the community communicate the accomplishments of the search conference and who will do it and to whom should they communicate it?

Coordination of the action-planning groups is an important task. Often a coordinating group forms at this point. Normally, this coordinating group is composed of someone from each action-planning group. It's the responsibility of the coordinating group to monitor implementation, keep the community informed through communications such as newsletters and e-mails, and see to it that the various strategies and action plans are in accord.

Once all these follow-up issues are settled, the search conference comes to a close. People walk away committed to action plans and next steps that are clear and compelling. They know they have accomplished a lot in a couple of days and realize the work is only now beginning. The fact that they have forged new relationships and created a new community in the search conference makes the future work seem achievable and important. People return to their workplaces and communities ready to spread their learning to others and make their desirable future a reality.

You can modify this basic search conference design to fit the needs of your system. People have successfully scanned the various layers of their task or business environment to better understand the effects of industry and regional changes on their organization. Others have done history as a timeline and recorded the key milestones and events for posterity. In some searches, people have added creativity to the most desirable system activity by encouraging groups to do skits, sing songs, and draw pictures of the future they want. There is no limit to the creativity you can use in a search conference.

We do have one user's warning, however. Some people have attempted to shorten the search conference to one day or a day and one half. They do this because they believe people will not come for the full two and one half days required of a full-blown search. While it is possible to cut short the search process and come up with action plans in a day, you risk sacrificing the community building necessary to ensure implementation. In shorter conferences, people don't walk away with a full understanding of what they have committed themselves to do, nor do they experience the bond with others that keeps the community together into the future.

In the next chapter, we apply the basic design described here to a real search conference. It's the search conference on the Nebraska mental health system. The Nebraska story brings to life all the elements of the basic design.

Chapter 2
Search
Conference
Design – the
Open Systems
Funnel

Chapter 3

The Nebraska Mental Health Search Conference

In this chapter, we present the story of the Nebraska mental health search conference. This search conference followed the basic design described in chapter 2. The story is told here to give you a vivid example of the step-by-step dynamics of a real search conference.

The state of Nebraska was settled over a century ago by pioneers moving west along the banks of the Platte River. Settlements popped up in the tracks of covered wagons – stops along the trail, places where people decided to stop moving and start farming. Later, the "iron horse" laid tracks and the population grew. Farming in Nebraska was and continues to be a vocation for the strong-willed. In the early days settlers were drawn together in communities to ensure their mutual survival. Self-reliance, independence, and resilience were cultural values. Political and social action from the beginning was simple and straightforward. Nebraska is the only state in the U.S. with a unicameral legislature – one legislative body with relatively direct access between citizens and politicians. What a great setting for a search conference!

Background–the Nebraska Adult Mental Health System

Dale Johnson, the head of the Nebraska Department of Public Institutions (DPI), decided to do a search conference to transform the state's adult mental health system in 1994. At the time of the search conference, mental health services were structured in the typical bureaucratic way, with control and coordination located at the state level, and flowing down the hierarchy to local care providers. Leaders at DPI were aware quite early of the changing nature of health care and the potential for health care reform. They could see the writing on the wall: reform would mean more direct, localized service delivery. They saw the search conference method as a way of getting ahead of the planning curve in a changing environment of health care delivery. DPI had a tradition of strategic planning, but had never involved people throughout the system to the extent feasible in the search conference. Previously they had just brought together mental health administrators from around the state to do inter-agency strategic planning. As a result of this meeting, administrators suggested DPI find a method to expand strategic planning in adult mental health services to a wider variety of people, including consumers, local private and public agencies, and direct care staff.

DPI leaders put together a small planning group to prepare for a search conference. This group limited its job to developing the purpose of the search conference and getting the right people there. They used the community reference system to select participants (see chapter 5 for more on the community reference system). The planning group asked key leaders in the mental health system to nominate people to participate in the conference. They then chose participants from this list, including mental health service-users. The planning group also decided what information they considered important for participants to have beforehand. This included material on the mental health system in Nebraska; recovering from mental illness, and the search conference process.

The search conference was held at a remote conference center on the grounds of the Arbor Day Farm in Nebraska City. This is the home of U.S. national Arbor Day, and is known for its beautiful arboretum. The center is designed along the lines of Frank Lloyd Wright architecture, an ideal setting for ecological learning. Inscribed on the wall near the entrance is Margaret Mead's inspirational quote: "Never underestimate the power of a small, committed group of citizens to change the world; indeed it is the only thing that ever has."

The search conference took place over two and one half days, beginning after dinner on a Tuesday evening in March 1994. The purpose of the search conference was: to bring together key people to develop shared commitment to specific action steps to build a unified mental health system driven by consumer needs.

The design of the conference looked like this:

Changes in the world

   Desirable and probable future of the world

     Changes in mental health care

       Appreciating our system's history

         What to keep, drop, create about our present system

           Most desirable Nebraska mental health system

             Strategies and actions

               Next steps for implementation

                 Presentation to officials

                   Implementation and diffusion of the plan

The Search Conference is Underway – Learning about the Environment

It was 7:30 pm Tuesday evening and the Nebraska mental health search conference was just underway. Administrators, managers, psychiatrists, health care providers, and consumers had arrived, and enjoyed a relaxed dinner together. There was a general welcome, briefing on the overall agenda and plan for the conference, and a discussion of participants' expectations.

Changes in the world

Without further fanfare, we were into the first search activity – a large-group brainstorm of changes in the world important for the future. The ground rules are simple: real data about changes in the world that have been happening over the past 5 to 7 years; all perceptions are valid; differences are OK. People began calling out real data about the world:

- ♦ The breakup of the Soviet Union
- ♦ Increased crime
- ♦ Global technology and communications
- ♦ The ozone layer
- ♦ AIDS epidemic spreading
- ♦ Increased volunteerism and involvement
- ♦ Loss of family values
- ♦ Increasing environmental disasters
- ♦ Increasing environmental stewardship
- ♦ Growing underclass and shift from east-west to north-south orientation
- ♦ Communication technologies
- ♦ Rapid change in the world
- ♦ Aging population
- ♦ Global hunger and poverty
- ♦ Drug abuse increasing
- ♦ More people need help

The list went on for thirty minutes. Conference facilitators recorded the words in straightforward fashion as they were spoken out loud. The wall was covered with important data about the world. Most everyone participated. Even those who did not speak were glued to the chart paper. It was a scene of high attention and participation. When everyone was satisfied that they had a comprehensive list of world changes, one of the conference facilitators commented that the list is this group's view of the real world, that it should stay up on the wall throughout the conference for all to consider, and that more items can be added by anyone anytime as long as they inform the larger community.

Desirable and probable future of the world

Next, people worked in small groups to identify and report the probable and desirable future of the world, ten years out. These ideals became the benchmark for developing the most desirable future of the system later in the conference.

Wednesday morning the group reconvened to finish working on the desirable and probable world and to continue through the search funnel. Here's a partial list of the desirable world the whole conference community agreed upon:

◆ People working together to solve global problems
◆ Available health care for everyone
◆ Sustainable global ecology
◆ Peaceful and nonviolent resolution of differences
◆ Better balance between individual and group rights

Changes in mental health care

In small groups, people identified key trends and changes in mental health important to consider in their planning. These were posted on the wall for everyone to see. From these small group outcomes, the large group picked the following changes as having the most impact on their system:

♦ Health care reform
♦ The move from hospitalization to community-based care
♦ Increased regulatory control
♦ Accountability of service providers
♦ Inadequate human and fiscal resources
♦ Changing demographics – aging population, urbanization, single parent families, increased cultural diversity, less affordable housing, increase in low income families
♦ Increasing voice among consumers, families, providers and advocates
♦ Consumers emerging as full partners – customer-service driven
♦ New technologies in treatment

Learning about the Nebraska Adult Mental Health System

Appreciating our system's history

It was now late morning. The conference community convened to look at the history of the mental health system. People sat in a large circle. The conference facilitators spelled out a few ground rules: several people may report about the same event – everyone's viewpoint is valid. We are here to listen. This session will take as long as it needs to take.

At first people used microphones so that everyone could hear the stories clearly. After a while, the level of listening in the room deepened and the microphones were put down and not needed anymore. There were emotional stories and events reported both by mental health consumers and providers who recalled the development of health care delivery, from earlier days of oppression and victimization to more humane practices now. One mental health consumer told how she was shackled and dragged away to the mental hospital years earlier and how degrading the experience was for her family. A man who had worked his way up the mental health system responded that he remembered handcuffing patients and forcing them from their homes as though he were a police officer. An important turning point, he noted, was the switch from a patient to a consumer or service-user orientation.

After this very intense history session, the group broke for a long lunch. The participants were encouraged to make use of the natural surroundings of the Arbor Day Farm. After lunch, small groups of people could be seen walking around the grounds, engrossed in conversation, getting to know each other, continuing the trust-building. After lunch a re-energized group of participants met to talk about the current mental health system.

What to keep, drop, create about our system
Once the group had a sense of what the system was like in the past, it was time to look at what the system looked like now. In a large group, participants called out what aspects of the mental health system as it is today they should keep the same, drop, or create. People became energized, especially in the create lists which covered over ten pieces of chart paper and included innovative and cutting-edge ideas for improving the system. These ideas would spark more creativity in the next activity, of planning the most desirable Nebraska mental health system.

Most desirable Nebraska mental health system
3:00 pm – time to move into the future. Small groups formed for this session, each group a reflection of the search community, made up of consumers, administrators, and staff. Working in these small groups, people created their most desirable future for the system. The instruction was to look ahead five years and come up with five vision points describing what the adult mental health system in Nebraska would look like. Five years was chosen for this activity as it was far enough into the future to be creative and free from the "shackles" of today's reality, and yet close enough in time for people to think that they would be able to actually do something to implement their plans.

Many of the groups used the beautiful surroundings of the conference center to help them envision what they wanted for the adult mental health system five years into the future. Walking on the tree-lined paths, sitting in the fragrant and lovely gardens, enabled deep discussions of the process for committing people to mental health centers, the difficulties for rural residents to have easy access to mental and health care, the challenges faced by consumers' families, and what should be done with regional centers (large, somewhat antiquated in- and out-patient facilities), and the like. The setting allowed both consumers and staff to say difficult things, to argue about, and mostly resolve issues they had.

Work on the desirable future lasted late into the night and finished up Thursday morning. This overnight time allowed people to talk and think about their visions outside of the structure of the group. People reported that they dreamt about their visions for mental health. People were energized and exhausted, then energized again. There was disagreement then agreement, as people found a vision they could all support. Some groups came in to work on Thursday morning and completely changed the direction they were going in, because of insights they'd gained through the overnight soak time. Having time through the night to think, dream, and ponder their visions made for a very energetic, enthusiastic start on Thursday.

Everyone listened intently as each group presented its vision of the most desirable future for adult mental health services in Nebraska. Questions were asked, points were clarified. When everyone felt they understood all of the desirable future vision points, it was time to integrate all of these points.

Each group cut its desirable future chart into strips, each containing one vision point. They took the vision point strips of paper to a large, blank wall and started to "clump" together those that were similar and leave those that were unique separate. If any points were in conflict, these were identified as well. The conference facilitators led a process to further integrate the vision points, with lots of questions for better understanding and some disagreement about what was really alike and what should stand alone.

A little time was spent determining whether the conflicting points could be clarified and resolved. However, deep conflicts were left for people to work on outside of this conference. At the end of this process there were fifteen clumps of desirable future vision points.

Once this clumping process was completed, it was time to prioritize the clumps to determine which ones to take to the action-planning phase. Each small group met again to identify three criteria against which to measure each vision-point clump. The groups used these criteria to rank each of the fifteen vision-point clumps and determine the top five. The groups reported on their criteria and their top five for the entire search community to see. Once all groups reported out, there was a list of the fifteen vision-point clumps, with check marks to show how many groups ranked each in the top five.

The integration process continued in the large group, talking through all the vision-point clumps to agree, or not, which ones would go to the strategy and action-plan phase of the conference – which ones would become the agreed, most desirable future for adult mental health in the state of Nebraska. Beginning with the clumps that received the most check marks in the previous activity, each point was discussed and clarified even further. Then the conference facilitators asked, "Should this be a part of your most desirable future?" At the end of an exhausting, but fruitful hour, the whole search community had agreed upon the final list of vision points – the ones they wanted to take forward into the future:

♦ Creation of a training and research institute
♦ New role for consumers – advocacy advisory bodies
♦ Revised role of the regional centers
♦ Refocusing the system to wellness

♦ Natural "shopping" regions to meet all mental health needs
♦ Comprehensive service delivery system
♦ Funding for all mental health services comes through one point
♦ Mental health benefits for all citizens – parity in mental health reform
♦ New commitment process
♦ System accountability – outcome measures

Action-planning

Strategies and actions

It was now time to translate these vision points into strategies and action plans. People formed new small groups based on the vision point they were interested in working, living, and planning for. At this point in the search conference, it became apparent that only the consumers had chosen to work on the vision point "new role for consumers – advocacy advisory bodies." At first this group was upset that there were no other participants interested in helping them work on this point, which was very important to them. After bemoaning this a bit, they decided that the best way for them to create a more visible advocacy/advisory role for consumers was to have at least two consumers in each of the other action-planning groups. This way they would be working on this vision point in an indirect but effective way. This left nine vision points to develop strategies and action plans for.

The other action-planning groups welcomed the new consumer members and brought them up to speed on the groups' planning work. Each group developed an action plan for their vision point. This work included:

♦ Clearly defining their vision point as a strategic goal statement
♦ Finding ways around key constraints to their strategic goal

♦ Specific action plans with short and long term timeframes, names of who is responsible for implementing, who needs to be involved, and measures for success

The action-planning work didn't finish until 9:00 pm Thursday night. Quitting time! However, most groups continued to work for a while longer, too enthusiastic to stop.

Friday morning dawned and a pretty exhausted, yet enthusiastic search community convened to finish the conference. The action-planning groups finalized their plans – at least as far as they could within the confines of the search conference. Groups needed to do research and add people to their planning group to help them. But for now they were at a point where they could say, "We're ready to report our plan."

Because there were nine action-planning groups, the conference facilitators decided that an "Action Fair" was the best way for each group to share their plans with the other members of the search community for clarification and feedback. This was important because each action-planning group was not working independently, but on behalf of the entire search community. Each group chose a member to stay with their plan to report it to the other groups, then each group rotated around the room, listening to the other groups' reports, asking questions for clarification, and getting feedback. The reporters rotated, as well, so they could hear most of the other plans. Time was given for the planning groups to discuss the feedback they had received and make any changes to their action plans based on the feedback and what they had heard about the others' plans. A brief report out allowed the groups to share any changes they had made to their plans. In the end, each action plan became the property of the whole search community.

Next steps to implementation

The search conference ended with an open large-group discussion of critical next steps to keep the momentum and commitment sparked in the conference going into the future. People committed to take the plans forward to implementation. Ways to disseminate the results of this conference to others in the system were determined. A group formed to communicate the progress of the action plans in a periodic newsletter. Another group came together to work on putting a presentation/action plan fair together, so that people who were involved in adult mental health in the state could view the action plans, ask questions, and give feedback.

The Director of the Department of Public Institutions agreed to convene the first meeting of the implementation/coordinating team. This group included representatives of each action-planning group. Its work was to meet regularly to check the progress that each group was making on implementing its plan, to discuss the resource needs of each group, to make sure that the groups were not working against each other, and to ensure that they were all going in the same direction – towards their most desirable future.

Presentation to officials

At the end of the conference several state government officials came to hear the results of the search conference. Participants took over control of the conference at this point and presented their outcomes to members of the governor's and legislative staffs.

The government officials who attended the closing session of the first search conference took back a positive message to governor Benjamin Nelson about the powerful outcomes of the conference. DPI leaders were pleased with the strategies and commitments developed at the search.

Benefits of the Search Conference

In addition to having a group of people committed to carrying out the action plans, participants at this search conference came away with some other benefits as well. In interviews done over a year later, several participants reported that relationships had changed as a result of the search conference. Comments included:

♦ The search environment created the opportunity to be open
♦ This open process considered all stakeholders' interests and gave an opportunity for the consumers to have a voice
♦ I liked the conference because it was a relief to deal with people away from the bureaucracy of my job
♦ We deal with each other differently after the search conference
♦ This allowed us to look at things in a visionary, global way. It opened up our horizons
♦ You don't know where you'll end up. It is an adventure. It gave the opportunity to be a part of something empowering
♦ It was safe, I could speak as a participant, not as a director

How an Action Plan Develops: From Strips of Paper Containing Vision Points to a Plan

At the end of the compiling and integration of points from the "most desirable future of Nebraska mental health" activity, one group took on seven strips of paper that had been clumped together under the vision point: system accountability – outcome measures. These strips of paper held the following words:

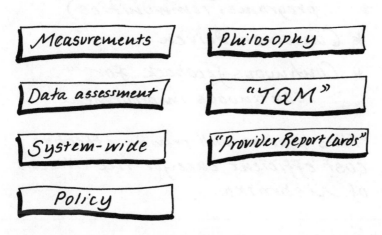

They also had all of the data from the other search activities, the conversations they had had in large and small groups, and their own knowledge about their topic and their system. They went to work.

The strategic goal statement
The group translated the above vision point (system accountability – outcome measures), along with the descriptive bullet points, into a clear goal statement that included all the rich conversations in large and small groups during the desirable future activities. This is what they came up with:

> # The Vision
> To create a flexible and ongoing performance improvement process which includes the following:
>
> * Commonly agreed upon key indicators
> * Multiple sources of data
> * Multi-level participation
>   (i.e. state, regions, consumers, programs, communities)
>
> * Consumer driven
>
> * Continuous feedback for continuous improvement
>
> This process will provide effective, cost efficient care for the citizens of Nebraska

They identified the following key constraints that might prevent them from implementing their strategic goal.

Key Constraints

A. • Win-Lose Attitude –
   Culturally & Institutionally

B. • Meaningless additional paperwork

C. ⊙ Need common language

D. • Agreement to participate

E. • Lack of mechanism that allows all
   to participate

F. • Power relationships shift

G. ⊙ No agreed upon measures
   of success

H. ⊙ Management Info System /
   data collection / data analysis

I. • Lack of skills to use data

J. • Individual (hidden) agendas

K. • Lack of knowledge of what TQM is

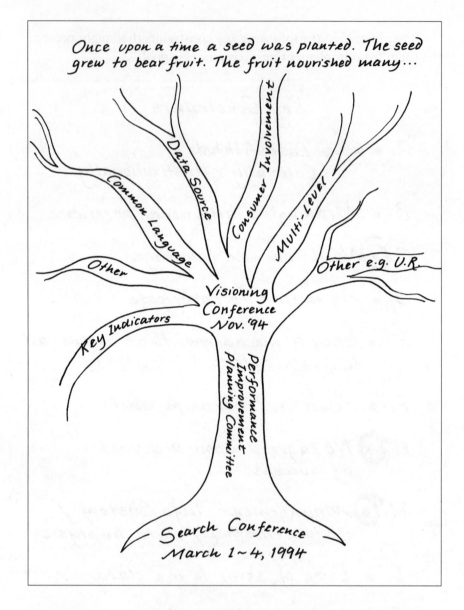

Once upon a time a seed was planted. The seed grew to bear fruit. The fruit nourished many...

Data Source

Consumer Involvement

Common Language

Multi-Level

Other

Other e.g. U.R.

Visioning Conference Nov. '94

Key Indicators

Performance Improvement Planning Committee

Search Conference March 1~4, 1994

Finding ways to deal with these constraints formed the basis of their action-planning. It led them to decide to do a search conference bringing all the key system performance players together.

The Action Plan

Strategy:

Visioning Conference to reach "consensus" followed by smaller work groups

Long Term:

Visioning Conference to be held by November 1, 1994, with the following purpose: To develop a shared commitment to specific action steps to build a unified, statewide performance improvement process

Short Term:

Planning Committee to meet by May 1, 1994 (to determine how funded, place, participants etc.)

The action plan

In addition to the long and short term goals, the action planning group identified who would be responsible for carrying each goal forward and how they would measure the successful implementation of each goal.

Long Term Goal:
Responsible persons: Performance Improvement Planning Committee
Measurements: Conference held; action plans developed

Short Term Goal:
Responsible persons: Staff support to be given to committee by Central Office Planning Department
Measurements: Committee Meets; Conference Plan Developed

Results
This action planning group was successful. The Performance Improvement Search Conference occurred in July 1994. This search community successfully agreed on a new performance improvement process for the mental health system and to five shared visions:

♦ Establishment of a Research, Training, and Evaluation Center
♦ Development of a Standard paperless Record
♦ Data Integration/Utilization
♦ Continuous Quality Improvement – Consumer Perspective
♦ Development of Performance Indicators for Children's Mental Health Services, Adult General Mental Health Services, and Adult Psychiatric Rehabilitation/Support Service

Conclusion

This performance improvement action plan was one of nine begun at the search conference. The groups that formed at the original conference continued to work on their plans, adding people whose expertise was needed, revising action steps and goals as necessary, changing the plans as the environment changed. For instance, in the middle of working on the plan for the revised role of the regional centers, the legislature in Nebraska enacted a mental health managed care law. This caused the regional centers planning group to change its focus to work on how the regional centers could serve citizens under managed care for mental health consumers.

State officials, administrators, and consumers were impressed with the process, the planning community, and the results of the adult mental health search conference. Later that year, a search conference on children's mental health was held. Staff members were trained in the search methodology. In subsequent years, several regions in Nebraska held search conferences to discover the most desirable future for services in their regions. Search had taken root in Nebraska.

Postscript

Several years after these search conferences, the state of Nebraska decided that it would be in the best interests of citizens to create a Department of Health and Human Services by merging five departments into one. The Department of Public Institutions was one of the five. DPI fostered the principle of participation during this restructuring process. Search conference principles were used to enable staff and users of the system to participate in the restructuring of Health and Human Services.

This chapter gave you an in-depth example of the basic search conference design. Next we will look at the simple, but deep principles and concepts that come to life in a search, whether in Nebraska or in your own organization or community.

Chapter 4

Principles at Work in Every Search Conference

Good cooks don't follow recipes, they use principles
Julia Child

Much of the thinking that underpins the search conference comes from the fields of psychology, ecology, and the social sciences. Fred Emery and Eric Trist, who "rediscovered" searching, and Merrelyn Emery, who has developed it since, drew on a wide variety of original research to offer some guiding principles deeply grounded in theory. And as Kurt Lewin, the founder of action research, said, "There is nothing so practical as a good theory."

To recap, the focus of a search is the task the group has to do in the future, but it is carefully structured to work on the emotional level too. Two things come out of a search conference:

♦ a plan for the most desirable future
♦ a newly formed community of people with energy and commitment to implement their plan.

The search therefore has power to energize and motivate individuals to do things they would rarely, if ever, contemplate alone.

What follows is an introduction to some of the thinking

behind the design of the search conference. Fred Emery talks of "rediscovering the search conference", and notes that it has been around in recognizable form for thousands of years. He mentions the descriptions of ancient Persian council meetings by Herodotus, and the Pathan institution of the "jirca".[1] Nelson Mandela's description of the tribal meetings of his youth in Thembuland also has much in common with search.

Fred Emery and Eric Trist ran the first search conference, as we now know it, in 1960 at Barford in Warwickshire UK. The Tavistock Institute for Human Relations, where they both worked, was asked to design a conference that would enable a successful merger between two rival companies with intensely different cultures, the Bristol and the Siddeley aero-engine companies. The new organization was riven with differences. It had no common strategic plan and there were two cultures contemptuous of each other. The weeklong course might have been another traditional "talking heads" conference where experts talked about their fields of expertise, but Emery and Trist believed a traditional conference of this type would have reinforced the dependency, passivity, and destructive behavior of the group. Instead, drawing on various research findings, they designed something very different: a weeklong conference with the clear task of producing a strategic plan. Emery and Trist spent six months designing this search conference for the twelve most senior people in both former organizations. Their starting point was the research of Solomon Asch (see below).

Creating Conditions for Open Dialogue

For the Barford search conference, Emery and Trist's first concern was how to create the conditions for dialogue. How do you create conditions where people who are not used to conversation, and who may start from a position of some hostility in such settings (as they did in Barford), feel free to contribute?

What they wanted at the end of the week was a group that had not only created a workable plan, but a group that had formed strong bonds and, most crucial of all, trusted each other. If this happened they knew they had the best chance to implement the plan. To get people to trust each other Emery and Trist relied on Solomon Asch's research on the conditions it takes for trust and open dialogue to occur among people. Asch's research identifies three crucial forerunners for building trust: [2]

In order for trust to develop, first *things need to be as they appear to be.* People need to feel able to be open about their knowledge, their opinions, and their feelings, and to take what other people say at face value. So, at Barford, Emery and Trist started by encouraging openness in whatever way they could. And still in the search conferences we run today, more than forty years later, all information is open, usually on flip charts. All small-group work is reported out into the room. In addition, people are actively encouraged to explore and check out what is being said. It becomes clear that difference in perception and opinion not only exist but are EXPECTED and VALUED. So people begin to feel they won't be excluded or scapegoated for expressing a different view. This encourages gradually increasing levels of honesty and openness. When participants see their words going up on the walls, and different people making presentations of small-group work, confidence grows that their contribution matters.

This condition for openness is already set in the preparation for the search when participants are briefed beforehand, so they know what to expect. There is a clear statement of the conference's agenda, purpose, and a discussion of participants' expectations.

The second thing Fred Emery and Eric Trist got from Asch and applied to the search conference was the *need people have to believe their perceptions are shared by others,* that they see the same things. Asch wrote at length about various experiments that showed a widespread and deep-seated (he believed hardwired) trait in people's needs to believe they share the same perceptions as others. He did a variety of experiments to show that, over time, people's perceptions tend to move closer to what they individually perceive to be a "group norm". There is a downside to this trait, however, that concerned Asch greatly: the fact that the group pressure to conform was so strong that people found it difficult to resist. Like Kurt Lewin before him, he was interested in what it took for a person to be autonomous and independent.

For Emery and Trist, the upside of this group-conformity trait was that it supported the group's discovery of its common ground. However, Emery also wanted people to be able to express differences and disagreement. To achieve this, openness helps, but Fred Emery later introduced a practical approach to managing conflict that encourages the different opinions to surface. That practical way is what he called "rationalization of conflict" (described later in this chapter). In a search conference the open data gathering and analysis at various stages enables people to see similar patterns and trends, and these provide evidence of their shared perceptions of the social context.

The third condition is that *people need to see that they share the same human concerns as others*. This perception of psychological similarity encourages the development of relationships and alliances. People naturally seek confirmation of their basic human similarities. Once we see that the behavior and motives of others are similar to ours, we begin to feel more confident in the possibility of working together on a shared future.

So early on in the search conference people look at their worst fears and their greatest dreams for the future of the planet. The first task is for people to state out loud changes they perceive in the world over the last 5-7 years, with the ground rule that all perceptions are valid. The data is listed publicly on flip chart papers as stated without manipulation. This snapshot of the changing world establishes that we all share perceptions of the state of the world. We share the same concerns and the same dreams about the future. These concerns and ideals transcend gender, ethnicity, geography, status, and age.

This happens within the first two hours of the search conference. At the explicit task level it forms essential contextual data for designing the future. At the implicit group-dynamic level, the barriers to dialogue start dissolving. There is no reference to group dynamics, no attempt to manage them, but it still works at the relationship level.

Trust starts to develop when people experience open dialogue where all views are welcome, where they can see they all share the perceptions of the world as well as the same worries and dreams. As this trust develops, relationships strengthen and deepen, increasing the likelihood of mutual learning and community building.

These conditions for dialogue are key features of a search conference. The successful implementation of the plan is directly linked to the strength of the relationships built up over the course of three days. The time it takes for these bonds to form is the major reason for the duration. The less time people have working on a common task, the less strong their relationships will be. The Barford search ran over a week, but Emery and Trist felt afterwards that was too long, that people got so involved that they experienced overload.

Open Systems Theory

Open systems theory now provides the most important principle underpinning the search conference, and contributes much to its effectiveness for designing and implementing sustainable change in our uncertain, turbulent world. The basic premise of open systems as developed by Fred Emery is that the world is made up of systems and environments. For any system to be successful, it needs to have an open, adaptive relationship with its environment. The diagram shows how this system-environment relationship works.

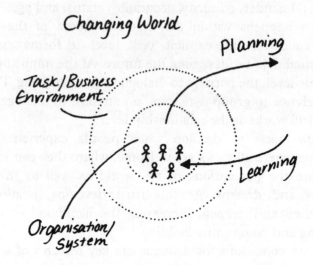

A system is everything inside the inner circle of the diagram. The system could be a company, a division within that company, an industry made up of many companies and stakeholders. Or a system could be a community or an important social issue in that community such as mental health, crime, or transportation. A system could also be an issue in a region, country, or international institution.

Environment is everything outside the boundary of the system, whatever the system is. The outer layer we call the changing world. The closer-in layer is the task or business environment just outside the system's boundaries – the larger company, competitors, regulators, and the larger industry. In order to survive and prosper, a system needs to open itself to learning from its environment (learning arrow coming in.) Based on what the system learns about its environment and what it knows about itself, the system plans for a future in which it will be adaptive (planning arrow going out.) Adaptive in this sense means the system and environment are in a constantly changing relationship in which the system is learning from and is affected by the environment and, likewise, the environment is also affected and changed by the system. It's a two-way street of mutual impact.

This is a bit different from the way the word "adaptive" is sometimes used. Today many define "adaptive" as accommodation to change. So many organizations are now trying to do more and react faster, just keep in step with changes that seem inevitable. We have a different take on this: humans can both be affected by and also *act to affect* their environment, making it more manageable. In the search conference we are trying to get a better grip on our environment and see what can be done to change it for the benefit of the system.

Today's global environment is turbulent, changing faster than institutions within it can handle. We now take this for granted, but it wasn't always this way. In the first half of the 20th century, the environment was more stable and predictable. Institutions such as large corporations and government organizations could plan for the future in a more traditional way, knowing that their plans were more under their control. Top management could invent strategic plans and use command and control to make them happen. These huge bureaucracies could get by with rigid, inflexible structures and planning processes. The current global environment started to heat up in the late fifties and early sixties. It was during this time that Eric Trist and Fred Emery coined the term "turbulent environment" after a famously turbulent airplane flight. Using this metaphor, they noted that the broad social environment was becoming increasingly turbulent and unpredictable. Long-range planning was becoming more and more difficult to pull off.

In the "old days" of the last century, planning was a thoroughly rational and top down exercise that was often turned over to the experts. As decades sped past and we entered the 21st century, new ways of planning have come to be needed. It wasn't enough to just have a plan that made sense. You also needed people who could both carry out the plan *and* do it in an adaptive way, changing and modifying the plan as the environment shifted. Going back to the open systems diagram above, it's as though the system were "bobbing and weaving" into the future, continuously learning, changing, and planning anew.

Planning in turbulent times calls for new tools to guide us into the future. These new tools are ideals. What makes humans unique in the world is that we are purposeful systems. We can consciously make things happen. In the search conference we learn about our turbulent world and realize it didn't happen by accident. For the most part, we created this world. With that realization, it becomes possible to believe that we can change it too. That's what happens in a search conference. People work together to discover the ideals they aspire to in the future and make action plans to get there. When people in a search conference work in small groups to analyze the changes they perceive happening in the world, they are going into an ideal-seeking state of mind. The task is to describe the most desirable world several years into the future.

In the Nebraska mental health system search conference described in chapter 3, these are some of the ideals that emerged as the group's most desirable world of the future:

♦ People working together to solve global problems
♦ Available health care for everyone
♦ Sustainable global ecology
♦ Peaceful and nonviolent resolution of differences
♦ Better balance between individual and group rights

Likewise, when people create their most desirable system in five years time, they are expressing their hopes and dreams for the future, ideals worth aspiring to and working to achieve. Then they translate these ideals into action. If you were to walk into a conference room where a search was happening, you would see walls covered with chart paper containing the results of the environmental scans and their analyses – changes in the world as well as changes in the business environment. There is a practical reason for this. Once the group has developed the system's most desirable future, people test their desirable future to see if it is adaptive in the world they perceived.

The search conference enables people to learn about their environment. What is changing in our environment? What's happening that we need to take account of when planning the future? Scanning the environment and making sense of what we find there is like exercising a muscle that has gone weak. The muscle in this case is the natural, innate human ability to sense our surroundings and, based on what we learn, to take action accordingly. This gives those in the search conference a new way of working that informs them and encourages them to notice and use environmental information in their planning both during and after the search. One participant reflected that, after experiencing the environmental scan and analysis, "Searching has become a way of seeing. My whole life has become a search conference."

The Democratic Design Principle: From Kurt Lewin to Fred Emery

Kurt Lewin was another vital influence on the development of the search conference. Fred Emery learned a great deal both from Lewin's research and also his belief that social science research should work to enhance the quality of our lives. The search conference embodies both:

> it is a way of doing action research, which enables people to design and implement a plan for a better future; and
> the democratic, participative way in which it does this is based on research findings of Kurt Lewin.

One of Kurt Lewin's most abiding pieces of research was on leadership and its effect on learning and behavior.[3] This research illustrated clearly that behavior is a function of the relationship between a person and the situation that person is in. Deprive people of responsibility and they will behave irresponsibly. Give them responsibility and they use it well.

In this groundbreaking research, young members of a boys' club made model airplanes with adults who used three leadership approaches – autocratic, laissez-faire, and democratic. In these leadership studies, the task of the groups of young people was to make model airplanes with an autocratic or democratic team leader. The researches discovered the laissez-faire style by accident when the adult leader just didn't know what to do and ended up doing nothing.

The autocratically-led and structured team produced low-quality planes, and the boys were not satisfied with the experience. Some planes were broken up afterwards. There was conflict in the group, scapegoating, bullying, and the strict leader had to be there all the time to maintain order and see that work was done.

The democratic leader started by structuring the task in helpful ways, so the boys learned the skills and could soon build the planes themselves, asking for help when needed, with the leader acting as a resource. Both satisfaction and productivity were high – the boys took their planes home proudly. They worked happily when the team leader was not there.

The laissez-faire leader sat back and read his newspaper, only responding to requests. There was both low productivity and low satisfaction.

Lewin's conclusion was that the democratic approach took learning, effort and skill. While the autocratic approach was familiar, it took time to develop skilled democratic leadership, and the disciplines for self-managing teams. It was easy, but ineffective to react by being just laissez-faire.

Fred Emery learned from Kurt Lewin's research on leadership style, and his own experience working with self-managing groups in the British coalmines, as well as other projects in Scandinavia. Emery suggested that an organization could be designed to get these behaviors to occur. It's a matter of choice whether you want an organization's structure to be autocratic or democratic. Instead of calling these leadership styles, Emery named them organizational design principles. We now call them the bureaucratic design principle and the democratic design principle.[4] Every search conference is actually a temporary work organization. As such, you have the choice of which design principle to use to design its structure.

The bureaucratic design principle

The bureaucratic design principle states that responsibility for control and coordination of work should be located at least one level above where the work occurs. The result is an organization where employees are cogs in a machine and each team will have a supervisor who in turn will have a manager right up the hierarchical tree. We call this a bureaucratic organization.

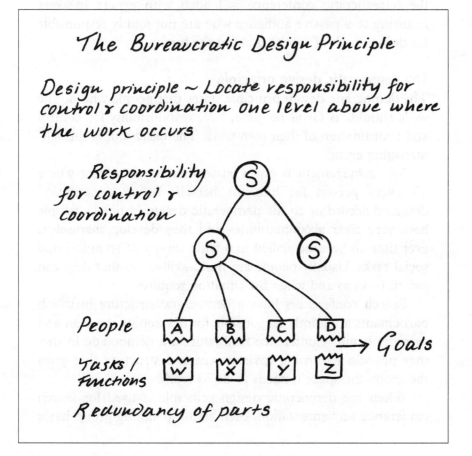

The Bureaucratic Design Principle

Design principle ~ Locate responsibility for control & coordination one level above where the work occurs

Responsibility for control & coordination

People

Tasks / Functions

Redundancy of parts

Goals

In this kind of organization, each person is treated like a replaceable part. When one part (person) fails, another takes over. An example is the traditional assembly line where a worker is limited to a segmented bit of work, and can be easily replaced by another worker who needs little, if any, training to do these simple tasks. The bureaucratic organization is composed of people whose skills are narrowly limited, and whose work is controlled and coordinated by supervisors. As a result, employees are frequently de-skilled and undervalued.

Applying this top down, bureaucratic design principle to the design of a conference results in "talking heads" conferences with poor implementation. We call it "talking heads" because the bureaucratic conference is loaded with expert speakers lecturing to a passive audience who are not jointly responsible for doing much of anything about the topic.

The democratic design principle

The democratic design principle states that people who do the work should, as far as possible, have responsibility for control and coordination of their own work. The basic unit is the self-managing group.

Self-management is not a laissez-faire environment where it's every person for him- or herself. In an organization designed according to the democratic design principle, people have very clear accountabilities and they develop themselves over time to become skilled in a wide variety of technical and social tasks. Usually people are multi-skilled, so that they can switch tasks as and when the situation requires.

Search conferences have a democratic structure in which participants are jointly responsible for developing the plan and carrying it out. Conference facilitators are democratic in that they provide a learning environment and structure that gives the group the space it needs to do its work.

When the democratic design principle is used for search conference implementation, each action-planning group has a

The Democratic Design Principle

Design principle ~ Locate responsibility for control & coordination with the people who do the work

Responsibility for control & coordination

Self managing team

Larger organisation

A B C D

→ Goals

Whole task/function

W X Y Z

Redundancy of functions

clear task, and individuals have choices to make about who does what and how. There is built-in flexibility. Groups try to keep both aligned to the overall task and attuned to what other groups are doing.

Groups in self-managing organizations are not autonomous. Their goals are still negotiated with the larger organization, and of course they are working with resources belonging to the larger organization. However, they are responsible for how they achieve their goals and this is what is so refreshingly different from a traditional working environment.

Similarly, self-managing action-planning groups that are implementing the search conference are not autonomous. Their goals are agreed with the search conference community and revised at review meetings. They are working on behalf of the whole community, and choose how best to achieve their particular task.

Creating Conditions for People to do Creative Work and not go into Fight-Flight or Dependency

From Fred Emery and Eric Trist's perspective in 1960 as experts at the Tavistock Institute, it was "theoretically inconceivable" that a group would stay creatively involved in its work for a whole week without going into dysfunctional behavior, either dependency or fight-flight. They based this belief on their colleague Wilfred Bion's earlier research into group dynamics with soldiers recovering during and after World War II.[5] Bion found that groups he was working with frequently went to great lengths to avoid their work. He spent years elaborating why it was that groups had such difficulty being functional and self-managing. Bion noted that groups form very easily and operate on two levels, one being the work mode where the group is focused on its task. However, at an unconscious level the group can also behave pathologically to avoid doing its work, perhaps especially if the work is disagreeable, unclear, or difficult in other ways. Bion identified three major ways in which this avoidance could manifest itself.

1. Dependency
Groups sometimes unconsciously assume the leader to be expert, to be almost godlike and invested with magical powers over them, a person who would also look after them. When this happened the group demonstrated passive behavior and was not interested in learning for themselves, as if saying, "Why not let the leader take care of us." The result was simple: the task did not get done.

2. Flight-fight

The group assumed there was an enemy inside or outside the group threatening them. Sometimes this was the leader who had fallen from grace. Other times opposing factions would emerge in the group, one against the other. The result: the group would either run away from or fight against their task or the leader. Once again, the group did not do much of its task.

3. Pairing

Here, people within the group formed pairs of different kinds. The group sometimes got preoccupied with a couple of people within the group who were developing a relationship that was seen as potentially useful, possibly in replacing the existing leader who was inadequate in some way. Bion considered this behavior to be pathological because it was distracting the group from its work.

Emery and Trist took several steps in designing the Barford search to ensure these unhelpful behaviors didn't happen. They wanted the group to go into and stay in what they called creative work mode. First, they set a clear and unambiguous task: a new strategic plan. This helped get the group into creative work. Emery did the upfront bit and Trist was in the background as group dynamics expert in case the group went into fight-flight or dependency. It didn't happen!

What Emery and Trist learned from the first search conference was the power of structure in guiding a group's behavior. By structure we mean the relationship between people and work they have to do – who is responsible for what. Using the democratic design principle to structure a search conference ensures that a group will go right into creative work mode and stay there, avoiding fight-flight and dependency. When the group has a clear and compelling task to do *and* they know they, and they alone, own that task, chances are better that they will do the work at hand.

Conferences and workshops designed along the lines of the bureaucratic design principle are those in which responsibility for learning is in the hands of the speaker. The audience assumes at an unconscious level that they are there to be taken care of by the speaker, that their job is to be dependent, passive listeners, not expected to take action.

Fight-flight is an active behavior, unlike the passivity of dependency. Conferences that move back and forth from bureaucratic to democratic design principle are likely to evoke fight-flight. You see it in workshops where there is a mixture of lecture and real work. A crisis of responsibility occurs. In one session the group is in charge of the task. Then in the next session the workshop leader is the expert responsible for imparting the learning and wisdom. The group responds with anxiety and may fight back against the task, or passively resist it. One reason we don't use training bits or have expert speakers in a search conference is that we want to keep the focus on the task and reduce the chances that the group will go into fight-flight.

In today's search conferences, participants are thoroughly responsible for all the work of the conference: data gathering, analysis, decision-making and action-planning. The conference facilitators provide an overall structure that is task-focused. Facilitators craft the tasks so that they are whole bits of work, allowing people to decide for themselves how to do the work. And facilitators negotiate each task of the conference with the whole group, making sure the task fits the purpose of the search conference.

A special word is in order about pairing. Over the years we have learned that pairing isn't necessarily negative. In today's search conferences we see pairing as potentially useful. At some time in your life you have probably been in a group meeting or training workshop in which two or more individuals put their heads together and started up a conversation, distracting or preventing the group from its task. How often have we seen the leader of such a group react by crushing the behavior of the pair, stopping it in its tracks? You can just as easily interpret this kind of pairing behavior as the spark of a new idea, instead of an attempt to overthrow the leader. Pairing rarely happens in a well-designed and well-run search conference. But when it does, we get excited because of the possibility that new energy is about to be unleashed and creative work will happen.

Ecological Learning

Fred Emery made another crucial contribution to the way we run search conferences. He trusted that people know what is happening around them and that they are capable of making the right decisions about what is in their best interests. The people in the search conference are the source of information – the experts. In Emery's words: "There is a real world and it is knowable to the ordinary person."

He based this on psychological research on perception and learning.[6] The research showed that people learn directly by continuously extracting meaning from perceived patterns. We sometimes call this "common sense". Emery called it "ecological learning". It is "ecological" in the sense that human systems have a relationship with their environment, where they are instinctively able to make sense of what is happening around them.

This is in sharp contrast to the school of thought still too prevalent in education today, which considers humans to be passive, empty vessels that need to be filled up with information from expert sources. In our view this is not the preferred way for people to learn and, furthermore, it reinforces dependency and the sense of external control.

Emery's approach turned out to have another useful result. In a rapidly changing world, it is virtually impossible for anyone to know everything that is going on. Put the right people together, each with their unique perception, knowledge, and experience, and you can map the complexity quickly. Do it this way and the picture that emerges stands a better chance of

♦ being up to date, and
♦ reflecting what is actually happening both inside and outside the system.

This is a pragmatic way to deal with turbulence and uncertainty, and another good reason for using a search conference to create change.

In a search conference people discover the rich information field in which they live, by seeing through their own and others' eyes and by trusting their perceptions rather than relying on the people we usually think of as experts. A search conference is a process where people use their innate abilities to make sense of their surrounding. It is learning by doing! As confidence grows and as we start exercising our atrophied sensing muscles, we become more perceptive and interested in learning. Indeed, the search conference builds the learning organization that everyone would ideally like.

We call this kind of learning "puzzle learning". The jigsaw puzzle is a useful metaphor. If you have ever opened a box containing a complex jigsaw puzzle and dumped the pieces on the table, then you know what a jumble you have to work with. The way to solve a jigsaw puzzle is to connect one piece with other pieces until a picture starts to take shape. This is ecological learning in that you look at the bits, trying them this way and that, until a pattern emerges. This is the way a search conference works. Each person comes with pieces of the overall puzzle and together they assemble it into the system's desirable future.

Puzzle learning makes sense in terms of data gathering for a complex system in a turbulent environment, and it also underlines the importance and usefulness of every person in the search conference being an expert in their own right. It reaffirms an individual's belief in him- or herself as a creative thinker and supports movement away from dependency on experts to solving our own problems through autonomy and self- management.

Rationalization of Conflict and Common Ground

 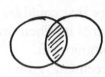 

Consensus   Common ground   Conflict

Fred Emery added this aspect some time after the Barford conference. It is something he discovered while running another search conference: focus energy on similarities and what is agreed (usually 85%) and *agree to disagree* about the rest. Fred and Merrelyn took the view that consensus decision-making was overrated, particularly as some differences are so deep they cannot be reconciled. The origins of this go back to 1965 when Fred Emery did an intervention in a territorial dispute between Singapore, Malaysia, and Indonesia–all still part of the British Empire at that time. All efforts at mediation had failed. Emery found that resolution of the conflict occurred once the parties shifted their attention to what they agreed on.[7]

We have already spoken about the fact that differences of opinion and perception are encouraged in a search conference. There can be disagreement too and this is welcome. So the focus in a search conference is discovering what we agree to and building on it. The idea is not to resolve conflict but to establish and enlarge our common ground agreement.

There is other research, not part of the development of the search conference, which is also useful in helping us understand conflict and common ground.[8] This research by futurist Edward Lindaman supports the notion that conflict is less likely when people in strategic planning exercises focus on developing a preferred future and then plan how to make it happen. This is in contrast to the depression and anxiety that happens when people try to solve problems. Instead of breaking a problem down and trying to solve it the old-fashioned way, try imagining a preferred future that could be a powerful guiding force attracting people towards it. When this happens, we have energy, enthusiasm, and commitment.

Common ground agreement grows when people are engaged in searching for their most desirable future and when they have spent days in open dialogue with each other about a system that matters to them. When disagreement does surface in a search conference, this is what to do:

Be sure to clarify the exact nature of the disagreement to make sure everyone *understands* it. This is why we call it rationalizing conflict. We want to make sure it is understood. Often this process of clarification uncovers that fact that it is not a difference at all but perhaps a matter of semantics.

Once it is clear that we have a real disagreement, two things are possible:

1. It goes directly onto a public disagreed list that stays up on the wall during the whole conference. The conflict is not shoved under the rug, but is respected and considered an important part of the system. The disagreement will live on and become a part of the community into the future. Or,

2. The search conference community delegates a small group to go off and try to resolve the disagreement in a relatively short, fixed, period of time while everyone else carries on.

An example of this occurred in the Hewlett Packard search

conference described briefly in chapter 1. It was time to agree on the plant's most desirable future and we hit a snag. People were disagreeing about which products to keep making and which to dump. The stakes were high as some of the managers in the room feared for their jobs if their product disappeared. The group could not tolerate leaving the item on the disagreed list because of the importance of the issue to the plant's future. Finally, a manager suggested that the whole group authorize five of its members to go off into another room and make a decision binding on all. After some discussion to clarify the task and choose the five people, they went off, leaving the rest to keep on working. A half hour later the group of five returned with their decision, and this was quickly accepted by the whole group.

Another example of how conflict was constructively addressed occurred in the Microsoft story told in chapter 9. In that case, clearly understanding the nature of the disagreements and respecting them led to the creation of a new organization that made perfect sense to all.

Our experience is that search conference communities do their best work when they don't get bogged down in disagreement and conflict, but focus their energy on what they want to happen together.

Summary

These six principles are at the core of what makes a search conference tick. Understanding them is the key to designing and running an effective search. When people have an open, safe environment in which to work, amazing things can happen. When the conference is structured along the lines of the democratic design principle, real work gets done and there is a minimum of dependency and fight-flight among participants. Making sure people pay close attention to the turbulent environment guarantees that the action plans will be adaptive and successful in that environment. Engaging people's common-sense learning produces a community of planners confident in themselves as the real experts. And treating conflict with respect while focusing on common ground is a healthy way to develop a community for any purpose. Use these guiding principles in designing and facilitating your search, and you will get the results you want.

Now that we better understand what happens in a search conference and why, it is time to look at all the steps that go into preparing the ground for a search conference on your system.

References

1 For more details on the background and history of the search conference see Emery, M. and Purser, R. *The Search Conference: A Powerful Method for Planning Organizational Change and Community Action.* San Francisco: Jossey-Bass Publishers, 1996.

2 Asch, Solomon. *Social Psychology.* Englewood Cliffs, N.J., 1952.

3 Lewin, Kurt. *Resolving Social Conflicts.* New York: Harper and Brothers, 1948.

4 Rehm, Robert. *People in Charge: Creating Self-Managing Workplaces.* Stroud, UK: Hawthorn Press, 1999.

5 Bion, Wilfred. *Experience in Groups.* New York: Basic Books, Inc., 1959.

6 Emery, M. (ed.) *Participative Design for Participative Democracy.* Canberra: Centre for Continuing Education, Australian National University, 1993.

7 See Emery, M. and Purser, R. *The Search Conference,* cited above.

8 Weisbord, Marvin. *Discovering Common Ground.* San Francisco: Berrett-Koehler, 1992.

Chapter 5

Preparing for a Search Conference

Preparation is key to the success of any important or challenging endeavor. Prior to going up to the mountains for a challenging trail ride, a horseback rider spends valuable time making sure all preparations are complete. The horse has to be healthy and without injury, the truck and trailer in good repair, the saddle and bridle in top-notch condition, and the saddle packs are full of all the necessary equipment and provisions. The trail has been researched to make sure it is scenic and safe for the ability of the horse and rider. The rider puts helmet on, mounts the horse, and the ride begins.

It's the same with a search conference. The quality of the outcome of a search conference is directly related to the care taken during the preparation phase of the search process. The more careful thought and consideration the better the end results. This does not mean that preparation has to take months, but it does need to be deliberate.

When preparation is done well, the conference gives birth to action plans that are well thought out and grounded in the system's relationship to the environment. These search conferences are a joy to follow up. When we call people who were in the conferences, we find they are excited about the work they are doing on the plans. Results of their action-planning groups are soon visible within and outside the system. Action-planning groups have grown as word of the search conference results is spread. New members have come on board with their skills, knowledge, and enthusiasm.

When search conferences are planned hastily or without careful thought and attention to detail, you run the risk of having the wrong people working on the wrong task. As a result, the action plans may not be clearly defined, a plan to spread and transmit the results of the conference may lack detail and energy, people lose interest, and the action-planning groups often get stuck and stop meeting.

When we think about preparing a search conference, three things come to mind:

♦ Defining the system that will be the subject of the search conference
♦ Discovering the reason why people will be coming together to search
♦ Selecting the people who will participate in the search conference

This work is the task of a small planning group working together with search conference managers to prepare for the search conference.

The Introduction

The telephone rings. At the other end is a manager who says, "I have heard about search conferences. I want to have one in my organization." Or it's a community leader saying, "We have a difficult issue to resolve in our area. I think we need a search conference." Thus it begins.

The caller is usually the potential sponsor of the search conference, the person in a leadership position who wonders whether a search conference is appropriate for his or her system. Now is the time for an in-depth conversation about what a search conference is, the principles that underlie it, and the kinds of results the sponsor would like to see. The person on the phone needs to get a sense of what is realistic to expect from a search conference – how the principles of the search will play out in the organization. The search conference manager also needs to get a sense of the organization, what it is experiencing, and the kind of outcome it may be expecting.

The discussion about principles is a key one. If the organization does not value participation in decision-making, this may not be the right methodology. If it is OK to have participation at some levels of the organization, then having a search conference with people from those levels may be appropriate. If they want to involve a cross-section of levels and functions, great! And they may want people from outside the system to participate as well. All of the above, and more, are things to discuss at an early, preparatory stage.

Search Conference Managers

In a search conference, participants are collectively responsible for tasks and outcomes. Conference managers (sometimes called facilitators) are responsible for making sure participants have the best design for their task, providing the best possible learning environment. Search conference design and management require knowledge of search principles, ability to design the conference by creatively matching these principles to the search task, and the skill to modify the design once the conference is underway.

Conference managers are normally consultants who come from outside the system. They need to be involved from the start of the conference planning process. Conference managers should not have a vested interest in the subject matter. However, they do need to immerse themselves in the system so they understand what people are talking about. The job of conference managers is limited to designing and leading the search conference – not becoming involved in the content.

Search conference managers work closely with the planning group responsible for preparing the system for a search conference. They join the planning group at its first meeting and educate people about the search conference process and principles. They help the planning group discuss the pros and cons, benefits and risks, of doing a search conference for their organization or community, making sure all their questions and concerns are addressed. Once fully educated, the planning group can go ahead and fully embrace doing a search conference. The conference managers also consult with the planning group on the design of the conference, making sure every activity fits the needs of the system.

The Planning Group

The sponsor convenes a small planning group to prepare the system for the search conference. Their major tasks are: to make sure that they identify the system under discussion in the search conference; to clearly define the purpose of the conference; and to get the right people to attend the conference. They are also involved in the logistical details of convening the event.

The size of the planning group varies from system to system. Sometimes, it makes sense for the manager and his or her management team to take on this task. This is especially true in organizations that are doing a search conference for developing a strategic plan, where the system is readily defined, the purpose statement clear, and the participants are easily identifiable. For example, the manager in the Hewlett Packard story from chapter 1 learned about the search conference, quickly called together his team, and the search conference took place two weeks later.

Normally, a small group comes together to do the

preparation. This can happen in a single organization search conference as well as one that spans several organizations or deals with a complex issue. Search conferences at the community level, especially ones around complex social issues, may have planning groups with as many as eight to ten people. Generally, the larger the planning group, the longer it takes to prepare.

The planning group should be a reflection of the system being searched. This means having people from different parts of the organization or community be part of the planning group. This allows the planning group to ensure they identify the right purpose for the search; they invite the right people to participate; and they get a sense of some of the issues that may be contentious in the conference. It is nice to know what one may be up against ahead of time! This does not mean that every group in the organization needs to be represented. Knowledge of the whole system needs to be in the room.

The work of the planning group is over when the search conference begins. Generally, they become participants in the conference, with no more responsibility for the outcome of the search than anyone else. Now the responsibility for running the conference falls on the shoulders of the search conference managers. The work of the planning group is integral to a successful outcome of the search process. When all the preparation has been thoroughly and effectively completed, the results of the conference are almost assured.

In preparing for a search conference in a medium-sized, urban school district in the U.S., the planning group was very carefully put together by the sponsor of the search conference, with consultation from search conference managers. Teachers, administrators, parents, and community members were invited to help prepare the event. A conflict was brewing in the school district between those who favored a return to "the basics" and those who preferred a more holistic approach to education. People from both sides of the conflict were invited to become members of the planning group. This was to ensure that the planning group understood all the aspects of this conflict and how this might play out in the search conference. This also allowed both groups to engage in the preparation and feel that they would be welcomed at the event. This planning group met for nine months prior to the search conference. During this time, conflicts were dealt with, trust was built, and the logistics were set up. When the search conference opened, the planning group was thanked for their invaluable work and the members became participants, with the same responsibilities as other participants.

Defining the System

As we have seen, systems can be of many kinds: organizations, social issues, departments, schools, communities, or geographic areas. In some cases, the system is simple to define. For example: the XXX Manufacturing Division of Hewlett Packard or the Tejano Charter School. Other times it can be complex: adult mental health in the State of Nebraska. Sometimes it is somewhere in the middle: the YYY Training Department, including customer, suppliers, and corporate representatives.

Defining the system is an important piece of work for the planning group. When one is in an event with a lot of people, it helps to be really clear about what it is that has brought all of them together. This becomes the focus of the search process. Using this system definition as a base, it is then possible to create a purpose statement for the search conference and determine who needs to be in the room to do the best planning for the future of the system.

System definitions have included: the adult mental health system in Nebraska, juvenile justice in the State of North Dakota, human resources at Microsoft, the Madison Benefits Company, prevention in the State of Colorado, the Tejano Charter School, the customers, staff, and contract trainers of the training department at Boeing.

Identifying the Search Conference Purpose

A clearly defined purpose statement is the focus of the search conference. Everything that happens in the event refers to, revolves around, and serves to further define this statement. Crafting it can be incredibly simple, such as "What is the most desirable future of our system?" Or it can be amazingly complex: "To work together to identify the goals we will achieve before the year 2000 in order to have each employee contribute to the business as if it were their own". In any case, the purpose statement incorporates the system definition and a phrase about a desirable future.

The purpose statement is used when people are invited to the event, when they are briefed prior to attending the event and many times during the conference itself. During the search conference, the purpose statement is displayed prominently on the wall where everyone can see it. The purpose statement is referenced before, during, and after the various activities in the conference. Each action plan uses the purpose statement as a screen – "Will implementation of our plan lead us towards our purpose statement?"

Developing the purpose statement is one of the main tasks of the planning group. Based on the complexity of the system and the complexity of the issues that are on the table, writing a purpose statement that everyone in the planning group agrees is the most appropriate one can take from five minutes to several hours. The simplest formula for a purpose statement is: "What is the most desirable future of X", when X is the definition of the system.

Examples of purpose statements include:

♦ Design a plan for the most desirable future of the AG Global HR Network that participants will carry out together.
♦ To create the most desirable future for the outbound experience at Denver International Airport.
♦ To work together to integrate what we learned last year into

Chapter 5
Preparing for a
Search
Conference

the most desirable future state for creating a work environment that ensures the future success of the people and businesses at _____.

♦ To bring together key people to set common goals for the delivery of services to those in the juvenile justice system.

♦ To develop policy choices for adult corrections in Oregon that make the most sense for the people of Oregon within fiscal constraints.

Selecting Participants

Once the planning group has defined the system and agreed on the purpose statement, the next task of the planning group is the selection of participants. They are chosen because they have important *knowledge about the system* and *can implement the plan* that comes out of the conference. If one thinks of the purpose statement and the system as a puzzle, the search conference is about puzzle-solving. Participants are selected because they carry pieces of the puzzle, through their knowledge, position, and interest. If a large piece of the puzzle is missing, the outcome of the search conference may be insufficient or the implementation difficult.

Choosing participants for a community search and an organization search can look very different. Generally, when doing a search conference in a community or on a social issue, use the community reference system method developed by Merrelyn Emery. The community reference system works in the following way:

1. Map out the social system – whether the system is a community issue, or industry. In the Denver juvenile justice summit described in chapter 1, the social system map included institutions such as education, law enforcement, courts, social services, and politics. The geographic boundary was the county line. And the map also showed

demographic information such as race, ethnicity, socioeconomic status, and crime statistics.

2. Determine the criteria for selecting people, such as knowledge of the system, decision-making authority, and potential for work on implementation.

3. Choose a person in each sector of the map and ask them for two or three names that fit the criteria. This is for input only; it is not an invitation at this point.

4. Ask each of the new names to give two or three names that fit the criteria.

5. After one or two repeats of this process, some of the same names should appear. Select these from the total list and add others to make sure that each piece in the system puzzle is included in the search community.

The community reference system clarifies that search conference participants are representative of some part of the system, but not there to represent anyone else's point of view, as they would be on a representative committee. They do not see themselves as stakeholders who are there to argue for and get the best deal for their constituents. They participate just as themselves.

For searches on the topic of strategic planning in corporate or public sector organizations, participants are normally the people, usually managers, who are responsible for the direction of the organization – the people who have collective knowledge of all the various parts of the system and who will be able to continue their involvement through the implementation of the action plan.

If the topic of the organization search conference is not strategic planning but planning for an organizational issue, such as the future of human resources, participation may be extended. Participants may be workers, people from corporate or division level, and various stakeholders, including customers and suppliers. The way you define the system governs who needs to be included in the search conference to ensure that people with knowledge of each piece of the organizational system puzzle is in the room.

Regardless of the system or purpose, experience teaches us that search conferences work best with between twenty and forty people, though we have successfully pushed that number up to fifty and beyond. The criterion is simple: face-to-face communication in which everyone can see and hear everyone else. This becomes critical when you come to that part of the search conference in which you are deciding on strategies and actions.

Briefing the Participants

Participants should be fully briefed about all aspects of the search conference beforehand. This is best done in a face-to-face meeting, so that all can fully understand what the search conference is and the purpose that they will be working towards. The briefing includes the conference purpose; an overview of the design; how people will work together; a bit about search conference principles; and the realization that participation doesn't stop at the end of the conference – action-planning groups live on into the future. This way, when people show up at the search conference, they know what to expect and are ready to get right to work. In systems where one part may not know a lot about the other part (as in a merger), or where there is a lot of conflict, there may need to be multiple briefings.

In some cases, the planning group determines that participants need to review certain information prior to the search conference, often called "pre-work". This can include demographic data, information about the industry, customer service surveys, information from the corporate or agency level, and research and other data pertinent to the topic at hand. This can be given to people through briefings or in writing. If the pre-work is in written form, it is good to give it to participants close to the date of the search conference, but with enough time for them to read the materials.

Logistics

Logistics includes finding the venue for the search conference, inviting participants, and making all the arrangements necessary to get people together for several days.

Venue. We prefer doing search conferences off-site and overnight. People need to plan in a space that allows real community to emerge. We call this kind of venue a "social island," a place where people can get away from the daily grind and the pressure of phone calls and e-mails. And it's important to schedule the search conference over the course of three days to ensure what we call "soak time" – time for people to chat about, think about, reflect on, and dream about the work going on during the search conference. In our experience it takes three days for a search community to come together as a community of action planners.

Putting everyone up at an expensive hotel is not always practical. If you can't do it, at least make sure you hold the search conference away from the worksite and do what you can to reduce the interference of work-related phone calls.

Inviting the participants. Most planning groups we have worked with invite participants by sending out a formal invitation – a letter describing the background, purpose, with details of time and place. People also need to know what they are committing to, particularly relating to commitment to follow-up the conference as members of action-planning groups. Members of the planning group typically follow these letters with phone calls to personalize the contact and make sure the invitation is clear and understandable.

The Meeting Room. The meeting room can be critical to the success of a search conference. It needs to be big enough for everyone to see all the participants, yet not so big that people cannot hear what is going on in the big group discussions. Theatre style rows of chairs and tables are not conducive to the open communication that happens in a search conference. Seating is best with chairs that can be arranged in small group circles, and then reconfigured easily to a large group conversation circle.

It is also important that the room have plenty of wall space for taping up chart paper. All the products of the search conference are publicly written on chart paper and put up on the walls for all to see and refer to over the three days. A free flow of refreshments helps too, and meals served buffet style. Search conferences do not follow rigid time-frames, making it inappropriate to schedule formal, predictable breaks. Make sure you have plenty of chart paper, easels, marking pens, and tape so that people can record their data and ideas with ease.

Summary
So the planning group has met for two or so months, the system is defined, the task is clear, the participants invited, and logistics settled. There are forty people sitting in a circle in a large room, with a clear understanding of why they are here, what they are to do. And they know the principles under which they will be working for the next three days. The planning group members have been thanked and taken off their planning-group hats. Their work as a planning group has successfully ended. They are now participants in the search conference. It is time to look at changes in the world. The search conference itself begins.

Chapter 6

After the Search: Co-creating the Desirable Future

In the end, all things have to be done
Goethe

So what happens after a search conference? How can participants best organize themselves to implement their desired future? And how can the planning group prepare the ground for implementation ahead of the search conference?

This chapter shows how to best organize action-planning groups and design a temporary organization for effective implementation of a search conference. This will help you consider how to prepare well ahead of time to make the most of the opportunities offered. A lack of attention to follow-up can undermine the results you want.

Search Follow-Up: Implementation Happens!

One of the triggers for Eric Trist's thinking about the benefits of participative planning took place in the 1930s, when he was visiting Hopi communities in the American southwest. He noticed that when there was a nationwide challenge or issue to tackle, the Hopi would get together for days to visit, celebrate, renew relationships, and also to discuss the issue that faced them. Over the days, and after many conversations, common ground would emerge around what they wanted. Then people would go home, and over the next months they would take actions on the basis of common understanding – apparently without what we would now call detailed action-planning.

Follow-up flows from what people sign up to do, how they engage others in this process, and how strongly the search community has built itself. In corporate and public sector organizations, search conferences build on an existing system, and result in a powerful community-building experience. For example, one British Post Office consultancy held a search to re-found itself. Almost all staff attended and enjoyed dancing together in the evening after the history story-telling session. They went away with a very clear understanding of their desired future, which the action-planning groups developed and presented to their senior management for clarification, approval and resourcing. It helped that most of the senior managers had fully participated in the search, and had already signed up. There is a strong likelihood of such organizational search conferences leading to effective implementation. This is already anticipated at the preparation stage when resources of time and a support team may already be in place for follow-up.

Community searches can be more challenging to implement, as participants may have busy family and working lives, with competing demands on their time. The system may be more complex, with different interests and agendas. Or the context may be difficult, such as the post civil war situation in the former Yugoslavia. For example, in November 1997, we managed a search conference at Illok near Vukovar in Eastern Croatia with 30 new members of the peace-building teams that were being set up by the Ossiek Centre for Peace. While they held a very successful search, we were concerned about their ability to organize themselves to carry out the work they wanted to do to create the desired future.

Many members of the peace teams had worked in state communist bureaucracies, hierarchical educational organizations, health organizations, or the army. Some were very used to command and control ways of working, while others reacted by wanting a laissez-faire, "anything goes" style of management. The command and control, bureaucratic way of organizing would have been inappropriate for their community development work, and the laissez-faire way ineffective. So we did a participative design workshop to set up the working peace teams and implement the services they were developing. (We describe in detail later in the chapter how the peace teams used the participative design workshop.)

One key outcome of the workshop was learning that such a participative, democratic way of working together for planning and organizing was itself a useful alternative model to both bureaucratic and laissez-faire approaches. However, we did not hear much from them for over two years, until we received an e-mail saying: "The search worked; the peace teams are established. We have learned a great deal. It has been very much action research in progress. The participative design of the follow-up was useful, but we have been so busy, we haven't had much time to reflect. So, please come back to coach us through planning and managing a series of search conferences for the communities we are working with!" The learning from this was that the search and participative design workshop had been the minimum they needed for implementation to happen.

Follow-up depends on the whole search process offering people the opportunity to engage, get on board, learn together, build relationships and create a common future that they want, based on shared ideals. Hurrying this can weaken commitment to follow-up. But equally, it is important to recognize that one third of the time in a search conference is spent in action-planning, so everyone goes away with a clear idea of the road ahead and what they have decided individually and collectively to do.

Chapter 6
After the
Search:
Co-creating
the Desirable
Future

Good Preparation Enables Effective Follow-Up

Implementation can founder because there is a lack of time and resources. So the planning group responsible for preparing the search conference needs to make sure there are enough resources for follow-up. For example, the planning group in one company agreed with managers and staff that the time demand for implementing the search was likely to be 10 days over 6 months. This was not an extra, or to be counted as overtime, but time that needed to be budgeted with extra resources. People are not infinite elastic bands whose time can be stretched to fit the extra demands.

This is also why it is important to invite people to a community search who have the time and energy for implementation. Diversity, different backgrounds, ages, a variety of occupations, roots in different parts of the community can all help here, rather than relying just on the usual community leaders. Often, there are people who are attracted to implementation projects because they see there is work to be done, rather than joining a group that is perceived to be just planning. For example, in a community search in the UK to set up a new performing arts center, one action plan was fund-raising. An action-planning group has taken on the task of running a monthly cabaret, called Brackets and Jam, where three sets of new performers can showcase their work to a receptive audience. It raises £200-500 each time, builds audiences, invites new people to get involved and offers specific tasks people can carry out, such as running the bar, publicity or lighting.

So in preparation, it is important to consider what follow-up resources are needed. Is there someone who can write up the search conference and action plans? Is there access to meeting space, office support, email, a web site, a budget for expenses, paid help and administration if needed? How can potential funders and stakeholders with resources be involved at this early stage? For example, with the performing arts center, several participants gave gifts and low interest or interest-free loans for the start-up and purchase costs.

Keep People Informed

The golden rule is: "Communicate!" Keeping people informed helps build commitment and practical involvement, because they can see the big picture and how their efforts are linked with others. This enables people to feel more responsible, take more ownership, and keep in contact.

Newsletters, email and websites help make communications effective. The newsletter can be mailed or e-mailed. Reports and the plans of action-planning groups can be posted on a website, and a chat room for dialogue. One search for waste management set up a process for dialogue whereby many different organizations with a stake in the plan responded by e-mail, and these replies were then integrated into the final plan. Regular get-togethers and review meetings further facilitate good communications.

Reconvening the original search conference for a half-day or evening review meeting enables new people to join, and the working groups to present:

♦ What they said they had planned to do
♦ What they have done
♦ With what success
♦ What help they need
♦ What they plan to do now

Chapter 8 tells the story of the Macatawa regional search conference in which the search community reconvened one year later to update its plan and enroll more people in the action.

The reconvened search conference community can do a quick environmental scan of the trends and changes in their context that need considering. This reawakens the capacity for taking effective action in a changing environment and helps make the most of the opportunities offered. They can then present their new plans, objectives, specify the support they need and get helpful feedback so as to continue to work on

Chapter 6
After the
Search:
Co-creating
the Desirable
Future

behalf of the whole search community. This process is a straightforward way of staying connected, keeping everyone informed, assessing progress and deciding what needs doing.[1]

Using Participative Design to Implement Search Conferences

The search conference is the middle part of an overall process that begins with preparation and ends with implementation. Every implementation process is different, and how the community organizes itself is crucial. Just letting things happen – the laissez-faire approach – is risky, for little may happen. Another danger is that action-planning groups become committees, with an overall committee structure. This can undermine the energy and motivation built up during the search conference, which was designed using the democratic design principle. Committees are typically bureaucratic structures in which responsibility for the agenda and action rests with the chairperson, not the whole group.

Either way – laissez-faire or committees – fails to continue to build on the participative working mode established by the search conference. One way to ensure the best possible organization for implementation is to use a participative design workshop, or PDW for short.

The participative design workshop is a method for enabling people to design democratic work structures and self-managing teams. It helps action-planning groups structure themselves on participative principles. You can use a participative design workshop either at the end of the search conference or within a month. The advantage of a PDW at the end of a search is that people go away with a clear structure and process to work with. However, participants may also be experiencing cognitive overload, and may need soak time for things to settle. So a break of a week or up to a month offers time for digestion, and participants can look forward to the participative design workshop.

Originally, Fred and Merrelyn Emery developed the participative design workshop for redesigning organizations from the traditional command and control organization to one structured by the democratic design principle.[2] This means that work is controlled and coordinated by the people doing the work, rather than the people at a level above.

Since the search conference is designed according to the democratic design principle, participants want to continue working in this way, controlling and coordinating their efforts, thus acting from common ground around their desired future. The participative design workshop can be used to support this, so that participants neither get frustrated by a laissez-faire, anything-goes approach, or a committee way of working.

You can use the following basic process to design a half-day or day participative design workshop to implement a search conference.[3] First, we present the workshop design. Then we give the example of a case study to show how it was used to set up the peace teams in Croatia. Here is the basic design of the participative design workshop as applied to a search conference community getting organized for action:

Purpose of the PDW: to create a self-managing organization for implementing the search conference desired future.

Phase 1: Analysis

- ♦ Briefing and discussion: What are the bureaucratic and the democratic design principles?
- ♦ Action-planning groups use the 6 criteria for productive work to analyze their previous experiences of action-planning.
- ♦ Report out – discussion: what helps and hinders productive work?
- ♦ Skills matrix: action-planning groups list the key skills needed to implement the action plans, and each group completes the skills matrix of who holds the relevant skills.

Chapter 6
After the
Search:
Co-creating
the Desirable
Future

Phase 2: Design
♦ Action-planning groups design a team structure for implementing their action plans.
♦ Report out to plenary and agree on final design.

Phase 3: Practicalities
Briefing: What is needed to build effective action-planning groups for implementation?

Each group works through the following questions, so they become a self-managing team:

♦ What are our team goals? What do we want to do, and how will we know when we have succeeded?
♦ What are our individual goals?
♦ How will we manage and coordinate our work? (Meetings, ground rules, how we will communicate with each other, who does what and when, recording decisions.)
♦ External relations: How will we consult and check with the other action-planning groups?
♦ What new skills do we need? Any training needs? (From the skills matrix in phase 1.)
♦ The resources we need: space, money, tools, equipment, etc.

Once the temporary organization of action-planning groups is designed, and each group is clear about how it will work, groups can work further on their action plans – who will do what, by when, to implement their plans. Groups can use the whole conference community to get feedback on their plans, take this feedback on board and then act on behalf of the whole.

Participative Design Workshop for Setting Up the Peace Teams

We return now to the Ossiek Centre for Peace search conference that set up peace teams. Here is how they used the participative design workshop to organize for action.

Purpose of the participative design workshop: to create a self-managing organization for implementing the peace team's desired future as agreed by the search conference.

Phase 1: Analysis

Briefing and discussion: What are the bureaucratic and the democratic design principles? What happens when these principles are used to design temporary organizations such as search conferences?

The peace teams were very interested in comparing and contrasting the two design principles, and had a clear understanding of the disadvantages of the bureaucratic design principle. However, it took longer to contrast the democratic design principle with the laissez-faire approach, which is really not a design principle at all. Kurt Lewin's research helped here, with the story of leadership studies of groups of young people who made model airplanes with leaders using three different approaches – autocratic, laissez-faire, and democratic. (The design principles and Kurt Lewin's research were discussed in chapter 4.)

Action-planning groups use the six criteria for productive work to analyze their previous experiences of action-planning (see box for explanation of the six criteria).

People work in small groups to complete the six criteria matrix. The purpose of this assessment is to explore to what extent people have experienced the six criteria for productive work in organizations or action-planning groups that they have experienced in the past.

In open group discussion, people rate how much of each

Chapter 6
After the
Search:
Co-creating
the Desirable
Future

criterion they experienced in a previous action-planning and implementation activity. If they have no such experience, then they rate satisfaction in their current or previous job.

Because the first three criteria need to be optimal for each individual, these three are scored from –5 (too little) to +5 (too much), with 0 being optimal, just right.

As the second three criteria are things you can never have too much of, they are scored from 0 (none) to 10 (lots).

The final group product will express the range of scores across the section. This activity normally takes about 45 minutes depending on the size of the group.

Example Matrix:

Psychological Criteria	Names of Participants				
	Branca	Sasha	Sanya	Karina	Igor
1. Elbow Room	–5	0	–4	–3	+5
2. Learning:					
(a) Setting goals	–4	+4	–2	–3	–3
(b) Getting feedback	–3	–4	0	–4	–4
3. Variety	–3	+4	0	+3	–5
4. Mutual Support & Respect	8	4	2	8	5
5. Meaningfulness:					
(a) Socially useful	9	9	8	9	6
(b) Seeing whole product/process	4	10	7	3	4
6. Desirable Future	3	8	5	2	2

The Six Criteria for Productive Work

Research has identified six human needs that should be satisfied for people to do productive work. We call these needs the six criteria for productive work. In order for an organization to be effective and deliver quality products and services, it has to be designed to satisfy these human needs. So, in implementing a search conference, it is important for people in action-planning groups to talk about how they can meet their needs while implementing their plan. The six criteria for productive work are:

1. Elbow-Room for Decision Making. People need to feel that they are their own bosses and that, except in exceptional circumstances, they have room to make decisions they can call their own. On the other hand, they do not need so much elbow-room that they just do not know what to do.

2. Opportunity to Learn On the Job and Go On Learning. Learning is a basic human need and activity. Even in leisure pursuits, people strive to constantly improve. Learning is possible only when people are able to:
a) Set goals that are reasonable challenges for them, and
b) Get feedback of results in time for them to correct their behaviour.

3. Variety. People need to be able to vary their work to avoid the extremes of boredom and fatigue. They need to set up a satisfying rhythm of work that provides enough variety and a reasonable challenge.

Chapter 6
After the
Search:
Co-creating
the Desirable
Future

4. Mutual Support and Respect. People need to be able to get help and respect from their co-workers. They need to avoid conditions where one person's gain is another's loss.

5. Meaningfulness. People need to be able to relate what they do and what they produce to their social life. Meaningfulness includes both the worth and quality of a product, and having a knowledge of the whole product. Many jobs lack meaning because workers see such a small part of the final product that its meaning is denied them.

Meaningfulness has two dimensions:

a) Socially useful,

and

b) Seeing whole product

Taken together, these dimensions make it possible for a person to see a real connection between their daily work and the world.

6. A Desirable Future. Put simply, people need work that leads to a desirable future for themselves, not a dead-end. This desirable future is not necessarily a promotion, but a career direction or move that will continue to allow personal growth and increase skills.

Self-managing action-planning groups directly address human needs at a structural level. Action-planning groups provide each of their members with the freedom to optimize their needs, to find the right balance of elbow-room, goal-setting, feedback, and variety. People provide back-up when someone is sick or away. They plan their own work and cover for each other. They allocate tasks to one another to ensure variety and to avoid individual boredom and fatigue. And they challenge one another to make a fair contribution.

Group vs. individual assessment

Practice what you preach when doing the assessment tasks in the workshop. This means being open and self-managing in all that you do, particularly in the way people complete the six criteria assessment. In the participative design workshop, the six criteria assessment is a group task. Everyone in the group sits around the flip chart discussing their own scores as they see them. They share their perceptions of other's scores, discussing and negotiating differences in perceptions, changing their scores if necessary. Together they arrive at a picture of how their previous experience of action-planning or their present workplace meets or fails to meet their needs. This approach features openness, cooperation, and a sense that we are all in the same boat together.

Report out and discussion: what helps and hinders productive work in action-planning groups?

There were very wide-ranging discussions in the peace teams, as previous experience was so diverse. Igor had had too much elbow-room in his previous job, low levels of feedback and opportunity for goal-setting, only moderate support and respect, and a limited future. He was looking for much more from the peace teams, especially support, skills leading to a desired future, and meaningful work.

This task really engaged participants, enabling them to talk about their experiences at work, in the army, at college – and to discuss what helps and hinders productive work when action-planning. Sharing this analysis and conversation in groups helped create a common language, deepened insight into individual differences and was a powerful team-building experience. They were keen to integrate the criteria for productive work into their work.

Chapter 6
After the
Search:
Co-creating
the Desirable
Future

Skills matrix: action-planning groups list the key skills needed to implement the action plans, and each group completes the skills matrix of who holds the relevant skill. People complete a matrix of skills that they currently hold that are connected in any way to implementing the search conference.

First, people list all the essential skills required in the action-planning group to make it work. Then, the groups compile a collective picture of their current skills by using a simple scale:

0 for none of a particular skill
One tick ✔ for a sufficient level of skill, or
Two ticks ✔✔ for high level of skill – which means this person can teach someone else

This activity can take an hour or more depending on the size of the group and the nature of the skills involved.

Example Matrix:

Essential Skills	Branca	Sasha	Sanya	Karina	Igor
A	✔✔	✔	0	0	0
B	✔	✔✔	✔	✔	✔✔
C	0	✔✔	✔✔	0	✔✔
D	✔	✔✔	✔✔	0	0
E	✔✔	✔	✔	0	✔

✔✔ = Can train   ✔ = Can do   0 = Cannot yet do

Essential skills such as administration, budgeting, target-setting, scheduling, publicity, handling the press, taking minutes are brainstormed down the left hand margin. In the case of the peace teams, there were also specific skills such as research, project skills, conflict resolution, reconciliation, knowledge of human rights issues, and so on. Groups analyzed their skills and were surprised at the rich resources they held individually and collectively.

99

Chapter 6
After the
Search:
Co-creating
the Desirable
Future

Phase 2: Designing the overall implementation structure

Action-planning groups design a team structure for implementing plans.

Here the group designed an overall structure for implementation with five teams for the geographical areas and communities the peace teams were engaged with. The design included a monthly review and planning meeting of all members in the first three months and a coordinating team. The coordinating team comprised a link person from each of the peace teams, who was to be rotated regularly. The design also included a coordinator who would negotiate plans, resources, and objectives with each of the teams, and support people for programs, administration, and resources. There was much discussion about the nature of work of peace teams in the field, and the work of the coordinating team – for example, how work was to be monitored, final selection for the teams, performance appraisal. This was worked out in practice over the first few months, with the different peace teams developing varying levels of self-management depending on competence and experience.

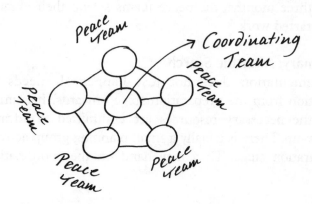

Phase 3: Practicalities

Briefing: What is needed to build effective action-planning groups for implementation?

Each action-planning group works through the following questions, so they become a self-managing team:

♦ What are our team goals? What do we want to do, and how will we know when we have succeeded? What is our work? What is not our work?

♦ What are our individual goals?

♦ What is our work plan? What will we do in the first three days, first three weeks, and first three months?

♦ How will we manage and coordinate our work? (Meetings, ground rules, how we will communicate with each other, who does what and when, recording decisions)

♦ External relations: How will we consult and check with the other action-planning groups, and the coordinating team?

♦ What skills do we have? What new skills do we need? Any training needs? (From the skills matrix.)

♦ The resources we need: space, money, transport, tools, equipment, etc.

Once the temporary organization of action-planning groups was designed, and each group was clear about the structure, the groups worked further on their action plans – who would do what, by when, to implement their plans. Groups used the conference community to get feedback on their plans. Over the next three months, the peace teams set up their organization and started work.[4]

Summary: After the Search

Implementation does not just happen. It needs careful attention from the preparation stage onwards. It is important that the necessary resources are committed in advance for follow-up. There is usually a small planning group active at the preparation stage. They may hand on the coordination and implementation task to a new group emerging from the search, making sure appropriate coordination and support continues.

The participative design workshop can be used to design a temporary organization of action-planning groups. This helps build the conference further with practical, self-managing tools and processes. As in the example of the peace teams, the PDW can also be used to both implement the search conference and to set up a new organization.

Chapter 6
After the
Search:
Co-creating
the Desirable
Future

References

1   Weisbord, M. and Janoff, S, *Future Search: An Action Guide to finding Common Ground in Organizations and Communities*, Berret-Kohler, San Francisco 1995. See pp. 193-194 for a helpful way of designing review meetings.

2   See Emery M. *Participative Design for Participative Democracy*, Centre for Continuing Education, Australian National University, Canberra, 1993, and Rehm, Robert, *People in Charge: Creating Self-Managing Workplaces*, Hawthorn Press, Stroud, UK 1999.

3   For an excellent, very thorough analysis of what helps and hinders effective implementation of search conferences, see Merrelyn Emery, "Organizing for the Successful Implementation of Planning: The Two Stage Model of Active Adaptation," unpublished paper, 1996.

4   The contribution of the Centar za Mir (Ossiek Peace Centre) peace teams' work to peace-building in East Slavonia is written up in the Oxford Research Groups report, see: "War Prevention Work: 50 Stories of People Resolving Conflict, Oxford, UK, 2001." Website address: www.oxfordresearchggroup.org.uk

Chapter 7
Critical Mass in Nebraska

It seems leaders everywhere are asking the same question in these turbulent, uncertain times: "How can we make change spread through our system and become sustainable?"

Organizations and communities often spend big money on change projects that result in great innovations, but these prove difficult to implement. Promises are made, such as: if you bring together lots of stakeholders and members of the system into a meeting or an event, change will happen. They often call on a concept called "critical mass" to prove their point. Get enough of the right people in the room at the same time for an event, and critical mass will occur. Well, not exactly! In our experience, critical mass takes more work than happens in a single event. The single event may be the spark, but critical mass is still some way down the road.

This is the story of how mental health leaders in the state of Nebraska spread the changes they sparked in their search conference. Here, critical mass theory meets Nebraska reality.

An Innovation in Nebraska's Mental Health System

Let's return to the Nebraska search conference story told in chapter 3. The search conference began the process of transforming the state's mental health system from a big, centralized bureaucracy to a client-driven, localized service. The state public mental health agency invited a variety of stakeholders to its search – service providers, doctors, leaders, politicians, users of mental health services, and workers in the system – about fifty people altogether. It was an emotional event. A sense of community began emerging the first day as people shared their experiences of living and working in a system that wasn't meeting anyone's needs. Clients told how they were poorly served, workers reported frustration with bureaucratic conditions, and leaders admitted not being able to work effectively across the system's rigid boundaries. Together participants forged a common ground future that shifted the state mental health system into a new locally-oriented model focused on client service delivery. It was a major innovation.

Towards the end of the conference, everyone worked diligently on a plan for spreading the innovation so that it would become real. They were energized and enthusiastic as they left the conference center. They were committed to go out and blitz the state with meetings, to get everyone – political leaders, mental health practitioners, and citizens at large – on board.

The first six months were tough going for this group. It was hard work at first. There were meetings with government leaders. They made presentations to groups of citizens throughout the state. Feedback was welcomed at these meetings and people were asked to help improve the plan. Meetings with mental health agency leaders happened too, in which professionals were asked to help implement the innovation.

At some point, about six months into the process, something strange began happening. People from the search conference started noticing that their work was becoming just a bit easier. The number of people adopting the innovation had grown considerably. The state executive and legislative branches were talking in positive tones about the innovation.

New legislation that supported the model started moving through legislative committees rapidly. Newspaper articles and editorials were favorable. Local mental health agencies were taking a quality view of their clients. And most surprising of all, people were cooperating across their once impermeable walls and boundaries. When they went back to research what had changed, people from the search conference said almost unanimously, "We are beginning to talk and behave together in fundamentally different ways than before."

What happened is that the state's new innovative plan for mental health had taken off – it had reached critical mass and now had a life of its own.

The Diffusion of Innovation

In his book *Diffusion of Innovations*, Everett Rogers defines diffusion as "the process by which an innovation is communicated through certain channels over time among the members of a social system."[1] For our purposes, an innovation is any new idea, organizational strategy, workplace design, or technology that people in your community or organization perceive as new. In this story, the diffusion was the state of Nebraska's new client-driven, localized mental health delivery model.

The leaders of the Nebraska mental health system used the search conference because they hoped involving lots of stakeholders in coming up with an innovative plan would speed implementation throughout the state. They wanted a quick rate of adoption. Rate of adoption, according to Rogers, is the speed with which members of a social system adopt an innovation. Research shows that there are certain perceived attributes of an innovation that explain the rate of its adoption.

A large percent of the differences in rate of adoption is explained by the following five attributes:

1. **Relative advantage** – the degree to which an innovation is perceived as being better than what preceded it. During the search conference people came up with a model that they thought was far superior to the present way. And because they were chosen to reflect the various parts of the system, including clients, people believed the innovation would be attractive to people throughout the state. And they were right!

2. **Compatibility** – the degree to which an innovation is perceived as consistent with the existing values, past experiences and needs of potential adopters. The search conference is a values-based planning method. People's desirable future reflects values they share in common. Nebraska is a down-to-earth, friendly, locally-focused culture. It has a history of pioneers coming across the rugged plains, settling down in farms and towns as they went west. It was easy to see that the new delivery model was compatible with the values and needs of people who would adopt it.

3. **Complexity** – the degree to which an innovation is perceived as relatively difficult to understand and use. The search conference participants succeeded in developing their plan and communication process so that it was direct and clear. As they went around the state making presentations, they continued to improve and clarify their model and message.

4. **Trialability** – the degree to which an innovation may be experimented with on a limited basis. When presenters went around the state, they invited local mental health agencies to try implementing their new model voluntarily.

5. **Observability** – the degree to which the results of an innovation are visible to others. Within one year, agencies began measuring client satisfaction and agencies were cooperating with one another.

Of course, rate of diffusion is a relative term. What's speedy for one person seems slow to another. In the Nebraska mental health environment, six months was lightning fast, considering the entrenched bureaucracy and deliberative state legislative processes. The fact that the innovation – the new state mental health model – scored positively on this scale of diffusion attributes helped create real critical mass.

Everett Rogers again: "Critical mass occurs at the point where enough people have adopted an innovation so that the innovation's further rate of adoption becomes self-sustaining." Self-sustaining means that the innovation takes off – it has a life of its own, with little need of pushing. Once critical mass occurs, the innovation may be almost impossible to stop.

The idea of critical mass came from physics, where it is defined as the amount of radioactive material necessary to produce a nuclear reaction. An atomic pile "goes critical" when a chain reaction of nuclear fission becomes self-sustaining. Once the pile goes critical, it cannot be stopped. Just like a nuclear reaction, interdependence occurs among people who adopt an innovation. Adopters influence other people to adopt by providing them with a positive evaluation of the innovation. Adopters spread the word, communicating their energy and enthusiasm for the innovation.

This kind of person-to-person influence usually makes the diffusion curve "take off" when somewhere between 5 percent and 20 percent of people in the system adopt the innovation. Unlike critical mass in a nuclear reaction, you cannot precisely measure critical mass in human systems. You can get a sense of it though. As in Nebraska, you can tell your innovation has taken off – reached critical mass – when it requires less effort to push the innovation. You will see people adopting the change all around you, rapidly and energetically.

As the diagram shows, once this take-off is achieved – the tipping point to critical mass – little additional promotion of the innovation is necessary. Further diffusion is self-generated by the innovation's own social momentum.

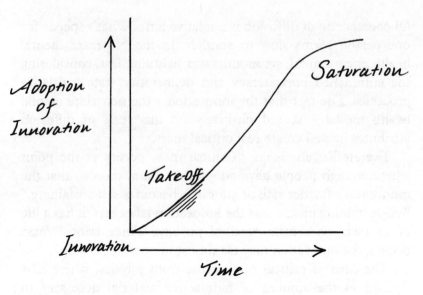

The Innovation Adoption Curve
(This diagram comes from materials developed by the
*   former Context Institute)*

Adopters fall into one or more of the following categories, depending on their reaction to the innovation being suggested:

1. **Innovators** – the venturesome 'idea people' whom you can find out front leading the way. The Nebraska search conference was full of innovative participants. We are not just talking about the system's leaders. Search conference organizers went to great lengths to make sure the ordinary citizens and mental health clients were also venturesome 'idea people' who would undertake to diffuse the plan through their networks and connections.

2. **Early adopters** – respected by others, these people are typically attracted to new ideas. Search conference participants sought out these people first when planning statewide presentations. It makes sense to get your

supporters informed and on-board as soon as you can. Early adopters tend to be good networkers and joiners.

3. **Early majority** – deliberate, open-minded, thoughtful, but definitely risk takers. You can expect about 1/3 of the people in a system to be in this category. This early majority category describes the citizenry of Nebraska at large. Presentations were made throughout the state to include feedback and new ideas from this large group of "early majority". They were critical to success.

4. **Late majority** – being skeptical, these people say, "Prove it to me". They account for another 1/3 of people in the system.

5. **Laggards** – attracted by whatever is traditional. Laggard doesn't mean they are bad, just resistant to the innovation being suggested. Not much energy was spent trying to convince "late majority" people and laggards. The major emphasis was on creating critical mass among the others in the state.

Diffusion of Innovation Learning Points

So, what can we learn from Nebraska's experience in diffusing their innovative mental health model? Here are the main points:

♦ Make sure you have innovators and leaders in your search conference – ordinary people as well as institutional leaders.

♦ Don't expect a single event to make change happen on its own. However, a search conference can produce the innovation that begins the journey to critical mass.

♦ Before you do a big event, plan for the real work to begin when the event is over. Have potential resources – people, time, money – all lined up.

♦ Don't let any grass grow between the timing of the event and the process that communicates the innovation to the rest of the system. Communicate immediately, using feedback meetings, the press, newsletters, or any channel of communication that will work in your system.

♦ Assess the innovation against the five "rate of adoption" attributes. If it proves negative, plan on a more difficult diffusion process that will take more time.

♦ Remember that critical mass is a physics theory. You can easily measure when you reach critical mass in a nuclear reaction – it's physics. Human systems are a different matter. It takes observation and judgment to see critical mass taking place in social change.

If you want your innovation to be sustained, start with a search conference that produces an innovation and a group of highly energized, enthusiastic people who are ready to lead the system to critical mass and beyond. When people create their own innovative plan, they are likely to have the level of commitment and energy to see it through.

Summary of Part One
In Part One we looked at the principles and detailed practice of search conferences, and saw how they can be an effective tool for change in many situations and systems. Part Two now retells some case histories of specific systems, illustrating how the search conference idea adapts to different needs.

Reference
1 Rogers, Everett M. *Diffusion of Innovation*. New York: Free Press, 1995.

Part Two:

Stories From
Search Conferences

Chapter 8

A Search Conference for Regional Planning: The Macatawa Story

by Frank Heckman

This is the story about how a local region in the state of Michigan USA used search conference methods over several years to create an integrated and comprehensive regional plan and some new ways of delivering it.

Background: Why Change an Old Dutch Settlement

Dutch immigrants settled the towns of Holland and Zeeland, Michigan, and the surrounding four townships along the banks of Lake Macatawa in the 1840s. The natural setting was similar in many ways to the landscape on the coast of their native Holland. Over the years, the city of Holland has grown and attracted certain industries, particularly furniture companies. Zeeland, on the other hand, remained small and conservative. Holland had been for many years a tourist stop for people, because of its small town charm, Dutch culture, and the annual Tulip Festival in May. Traditional Christian values have always permeated the area, particularly devotion to family, community, and simple living.

The Macatawa area was probably one of the healthiest economic climates in the state of Michigan. The area's solid work ethic, abundant resources and quality of life attracted new industries. For long it has been the home for outstanding companies such as the Prince Corporation, Haworth, Herman Miller, Beverage America, Bil-mar, and Heinz. Residents of the Macatawa area own the vast majority of these big companies. Direct, local feedback by their neighbors on how their businesses affect the community, as well as their own direct perception, has helped them face a wide range of social, economic, and ecological issues as resident citizens and businesses. Keeping loyal to the area's long-standing tradition of social responsibility, many of them have in the past reached out to help.

This all sounds as if we were describing heaven, not Holland, Michigan. But with a healthy, growing economy came increasing complexity – many new relationships and problems more associated with big cities than with small town Michigan. Increasingly, a growing population and changes in its cultural mix created both multiple demands and calls for new responses from the social, economic, political, and physical infrastructures of the area. Some of these trends included:

- ◆ A projected population increase of around 50 per cent by 2010
- ◆ Growing Hispanic and Asian populations in a conventional Dutch culture
- ◆ The beginning of gang and drug-related problems
- ◆ Lack of affordable and adequate housing
- ◆ Increasing language barriers
- ◆ Transportation problems that required comprehensive study and solutions

The need for more regional solutions and rising concern for the quality of life in the Macatawa area sparked the idea of doing a comprehensive regional planning process to help get a better handle on the future. For the first time, people in the community realized that there was both the need and opportunity to move beyond piecemeal solutions. Working together through the search conference would enable them to select and move toward a more desirable future.

How it Started

In 1993, community leaders formed a new organization called the Macatawa Area Coordinating Council (MACC). It encompassed the cities of Holland and Zeeland, and the townships of Holland, Park, Laketown, and Fillmore. The purpose of the council was to provide a new, cooperative framework for regional planning. The newly appointed council knew planning was the key to managing their future. They considered both a traditional, expert urban planning process and the search conference. They liked the search conference because of its potential for broad citizen and leadership involvement across the communities, and because they believed the event would produce a plan that people would be committed to implementing.

The council put together a small planning group made up of some of its members and other leaders in the community. The membership included a mayor, county politician, university leaders, a church leader, and business people. They limited their task to developing the purpose of the search conference, communicating it to the community, and designing a fair and reasonable way to attract the right participants. The group invited leaders from the entire area to a special reception at the local Holiday Inn where they introduced the search conference idea. They flashed the conference purpose up on the overhead projector:

115

Chapter 8
A Search
Conference for
Regional
Planning:
The Macatawa
Story

> "A gathering of the diverse people of the Macatawa area in a collaborative quest to create a common vision and develop paths to a significant future."

The planning group then led people through a process of identifying, right on the spot, those people whose participation would be critical for the success of the conference. Rich vander Broek, a planning group member and chair of MACC, recalls:

> "It was a gruelling selection process, in which our committee took a great deal of effort and time to formulate a slice of our community that was representative of income, age, culture, religion, the education and business community, and so forth. The reception informed community members about the upcoming search event and laid out the participant selection criteria that included the limits to the group size of the search conference, diversity, area-wide representation, and ability to contribute to the process (not just those three days in May, but also what was to follow during implementation). In all, three months later 63 people met at the Big Rapids search conference, and Maria Cruz reminded us: 'I was able to see the different roles in the community. For myself, I was a student, Hispanic and a female. So age, diversity, and gender were all there!'"

The First Macatawa Search Conference

In the late afternoon of Tuesday, May 24, 1994, participants started to pour in as they prepared themselves for their first evening session. Freedom from phone calls and other distractions truly made this search conference a two and one half day social island.

The search conference design looked like this:

Chapter 8
A Search
Conference for
Regional
Planning:
The Macatawa
Story

```
Changes in the world

    Probable and desirable future of the world

    Changes directly affecting Macatawa area

        History of our community

        Current assessment of our community

            Most desirable future of Macatawa

            Strategies and action plans

                Next steps

                Diffusion back to the community

                Implementation of the plan
```

Looking outside Macatawa: data-gathering and analysis about the context

After the orientation, introductions, and listing of hopes and expectations for the conference, the group began by brainstorming a long list of the significant changes in the world they believed would have an impact on their future. The wall was quickly covered with statements and phrases, such as: evolution of new culture, emphasis on speed, breakdown in family structure, medical advances, population explosion, people in ethnic conflicts, both spouses working, different religious traditions, aging population.

Participants were beginning to see their community in a much larger context. Later, when the large group discussed shared ideals, gender issues flared up. It was then the conference facilitators knew the lid was off the jar and from this point on the Macatawa people owned the search. The search conference facilitators, impressed by the boost of energy during the first evening session, heard participants saying as they left the room, "The gender discussion was great and long overdue!"

The next morning the group progressed by exploring the direct effects that changes in their immediate environment would have on them. Increased awareness of regional identity, land use pressures, employment-based changes, school-to-work transitions, competition, cultural shifts, and non-funded mandates were a few of the stress factors on the community that people identified. This direct environmental impact scan, coupled with the previous night's analysis of the changes in the world, helped the group see and understand the correlation between the outside world and the future direction of their community. All these meaningful and sometimes painful deliberations had implications for, and would bear fruit during, the planning of the most desirable future of the Macatawa area.

Looking back: history of Macatawa region

It was then time to move within the boundaries of the system and to appreciate its history and present functioning. The entire group pushed and pulled chairs closer to the center of the room for they knew they didn't want to miss any of the stories that made this community what it was that day. One of the community elders began:

> "I believe the foundation of who we are today was laid way back when the Dutch Reverend Van Raalte and the first settlers struck down on the shores of Lake Michigan. They had, through their oppression in Europe, strong feelings about religious freedom, hard and honest work, good education, and the fine relationship between owners and workers."

Others continued as time and space barriers dissolve:

> "The quarreling between the two Dutch settler towns and the fire in downtown Holland in 1872."

> "The building of the civic center some fifty years ago brought people socially together."

> "The evolving of the farming and fruit belt introduced the migrant Hispanic workers to the area, and this eventually led to more ethnic diversity."

> "In the late 1950s thirteen individual school systems joined to become a separate district."

> "The massive industry growth over the last twenty years: Haworth and Herman Miller for example."

> "The Hispanic and Laotian festivals, we are now celebrating many cultures."

> "The growth on the north side of Holland – malls, the public parks and beaches, railroad, ships, and hotels to attract people to the area."

> "And don't forget: we owe our name to the respected Chief Macatawa from the Ottawa tribe."

At the end a person said,

> "This is a very moving experience; I've learned more about the importance of our own history in this past hour than in the last forty years."

Chapter 8
A Search
Conference for
Regional
Planning:
The Macatawa
Story

Analysis of the Macatawa region as it currently stands

As people re-entered the room after lunch, three flip charts faced them, labeled: Keep, Drop, and Create. The conference facilitators could barely keep up the writing as people energetically assessed their present state of affairs and called out:

Keep:
+ Local control over industry
+ Tax abatement for business attraction
+ The stop sign at 17th Street

Drop:
+ Duplication of services in township fire and police departments
+ Tax abatements
+ The "if you are not Dutch, you are not much" attitude

The next list outperformed the other two by far; it read:

Create:
+ Consistency in land development
+ An effective area-wide public transportation system
+ A way for businesses to address childcare for their employees
+ A response to increased youth violence and gang issues
+ Enhance mechanisms for volunteerism in the community
+ A Spanish page in the local newspaper
+ More equitable funding among and across cities and townships

The Keep, Drop, and Create lists filled pages of chart paper and went up on the wall.

The future of Macatawa region

After a recap of the work they had already done, one of the conference facilitators put the search community on task with this instruction:

"In no more than five statements clearly describe the most desirable future for the Macatawa area by 1999."

Participants gathered in small, diverse groups to review the critical data on the walls, to dream large, be practical, think originally and present to the community their view on the most desirable future. After the small groups reported their future visions, a few people begin 'cutting and pasting' to integrate the thirty statements into a common list.

Common ground for the future

The entire community was now engaged in a discussion of what statements can or cannot be merged, which ones definitely stand alone, making absolutely clear the different points of view on the future of Macatawa. When this affinity process was done, the final list contained thirteen different statements.

The small groups again retreated to define three criteria to prioritize the list and rank the top five. This helped to identify where the community was willing to put its energy, and what future it truly wanted to work for. Debate, discussion, and finally agreement brought their future to light. Finally, the Macatawa search community came to closure:

Chapter 8
A Search
Conference for
Regional
Planning:
The Macatawa
Story

> We, as a community, are committed to improving the quality of life in the greater Macatawa area through creative, cooperative, and comprehensive work in the following eight areas: economic development, lifelong learning, environment, personal safety, healthcare, residential life, land use and transportation, and social services.

The next step was the planning.

Action-planning: making it happen

The search conference is as much about strategy as it is about making democratic choices. It aims beyond just having ideas and visions to making the desirable future happen. Action-planning is such a critical element that at least a third of the time is reserved for it. So the next morning, people chose one of the eight action areas listed above, the one they were most interested in developing strategies for, and they organized themselves into action priority groups accordingly.

They spent most of the third day developing their action areas: defining them in sufficient detail, identifying barriers and how to overcome them and planning milestones and next steps.

The camera of the local cable station zoomed in as the land group reported on how they would develop a coordinated and comprehensive land use strategy incorporating infrastructure systems inclusive of all the governmental units in the Macatawa area. In great detail they explained what it was they were going after, who would be involved, who would be responsible and by when. The community had some questions for clarification and provided feedback. They all applauded the fruits of intense and hard work. Each group took its turn reporting back the strategies they had spent most of the day developing, getting feedback.

Closing: back to the world

"The MACC is willing to provide this search community with all the support and resources that we have at our disposal. We are not here to receive the results of this conference. They are yours," said Sue Higgins, conference participant and director of MACC. She continued her commentary by saying, "It is the community's responsibility to control and coordinate our work as we set out to attain our future goals."

As a bottom-up support system the MACC avoided the trap of creating another bureaucracy. Volunteers from each action priority group formed a coordinating group. They acted as a clearing house to ease access to the different action groups, to disperse information on progress, and to respond to specific needs during implementation.

Suddenly we were at the end of the search conference. One participant summed it up well as he spoke into the camera: "It gave me great joy to be part of this because I've been involved with so many organizations and committees that have no idea and don't even care about what is going on in the community. They have no compassion and no sensitivity. I'm proud to have been part of this search conference."

Chapter 8
A Search
Conference for
Regional
Planning:
The Macatawa
Story

Immediately afterwards

Within months of the event, the MACC formally adopted the strategies as their strategic plan and restructured the council to support implementation of the eight strategies. The new MACC was now organized around the eight priority groups, with non-council search conference participants continuing to participate on each of these groups.

One year later

On a sunny May morning in 1995, one hundred and ten people gathered in Christ Memorial Church in Holland, Michigan to attend the second annual Macatawa search event. The agenda for the day was to review last year's achievements, to reassess the long-range desired future for Macatawa, and to establish priorities for the coming year. This day had been planned for a year and was part of the follow-up and diffusion of the original work the previous year.

For the second search, the large meeting space of the Christ Memorial Church was transformed into a science fair-type exhibition complete with visual displays, videos, and an array of other artifacts. The eight action priority groups that first formed at the end of the first search conference a year earlier, presented the year's accomplishments, along with stories of how they overcame obstacles. At the same time, the action groups got plenty of feedback on their work through small group discussions.

Here's a summary of three (of the eight) reports we had:

1. Macatawa's environmental action team report
Greg Holcombe from the environmental action group explains:

> "We defined our purpose on the environment: to initiate actions to identify and preserve sensitive and unique natural features and properties within the greater Lake Macatawa watershed for public enjoyment, use, and accessibility. The overall goal of this effort is to create and protect a Greenway Network in the Macatawa region. This network will be an interconnected system of public and private parks, forests, streams, and other open, undeveloped lands. These areas will be connected along Lake Macatawa tributaries by greenways that will provide corridors for use by citizens and wildlife."

Holcombe continued:

> "Inspired by the great parks and open spaces in this country, such as Grant Park, Lincoln Park, and the Forest Preserves in Chicago, our first goal was to map all the property that would compose the aspired Greenway Network." Holcombe then pointed to the large Macatawa Greenway Network map they constructed during the year.

> "Our next challenge," Holcombe noted, "was to determine how these core properties would be formed into the network by interconnecting them with Macatawa river tributaries."

You may be saying to yourself now, "This sounds like any planner's report; what's the big deal?" The essential difference is that Greg Holcombe is not a professional planner – he is a volunteer!

2. The personal safety group cites progress on a number of fronts

The next group is one working on personal safety. Here we see Bridgett Staub and Sgt. Gene Koopman reporting and asking for support on the personal safety action group. Bridgett explains what they have been doing:

> "A task force has been established to combat gang violence with the help of a computer database to track gang-related activity. There is increased street-level law enforcement in targeted neighborhoods. Prevention programs are working to strengthen police-school relationships, train community members to deal with juvenile crime, and provide parenting education. Safe haven sites have opened at community education buildings in targeted neighborhoods. Human services agencies are coordinating their activities to maximize availability to residents. And neighborhood restoration efforts, including repairs and paint blitzes, are helping to overcome deterioration."

Sgt. Gene Koopman stated publicly,

> "In spite of the obstacles we still need to overcome, this year has clearly been the best experience in my twenty years with the police force."

3. A breakthrough in healthcare

Moving along to the next presentation, the healthcare priority group reported breaking ground in its effort to coordinate healthcare and medical services in the entire area. They had been the driving force behind getting the community hospitals of Holland and Zeeland to think in terms of partnership and begin reducing redundant services. Lynn Kotecki explained enthusiastically: "Our next goal is to organize a search conference on healthcare as a way to get all the right people in

Chapter 8
A Search
Conference for
Regional
Planning:
The Macatawa
Story

the room and knock down the barriers that hinder the changes we so desperately need."

Finally

These are just three of the exciting achievements that the eight action priority groups presented in May 1995. People spent the rest of the day in small groups and plenary discussions around the feedback, evaluating current actions against the changing world, and in response to that, setting up new action groups. People generated many new initiatives, most of which were absorbed by the existing action priority groups. By the end of the day the group added a ninth group: the community access and technology group.

Chapter 9

Splitting System Principles at Microsoft: How Rationalizing Conflict Turned One System into Two

by Kevin Purcell and Robert Rehm

This is the story of one search conference out of several done by the Microsoft Products Groups. The Products Groups build the software that is the core of Microsoft's business. This search conference is interesting because it is about the practical application of two concepts – the system principle and rationalization of conflict – and how these concepts played out in real life, resulting in a creative solution nobody expected.

Microsoft has been using search conferences for several years, mainly for product planning purposes.[1] Much is known about Microsoft – about the work ethic, youthful energy of its workforce, its fast pace, and prevailing entrepreneurial spirit. Why would the world's leading hi-tech software developer go head over heels for the world's most low-tech participative planning method – the search conference?

The reason is simple. It's the Microsoft culture. One key aspect of the culture is the value the company places on direct, open discussion across boundaries – up, down, and across the organization. The search conference fits Microsoft culture because it's a practical way for a group to meet face-to-face and agree on an outcome they desire – creative plans for making creative products.

The search conference

This particular product group is made up of creative people from different fields – producers, editors, film industry people, designers from art schools around the world, and marketing people.

Before the search conference, product plans were in place, but they were not good enough, and the group was being asked to do too many different things at the same time. Similar products were being done in several places in Microsoft and they each had a different strategy. The group was also dealing with a set of dynamic markets new to Microsoft. This combined context of ever-changing segmented markets and lack of planning focus caused this product group to look for a new way to do integrated product planning.

The product group looked at several ways to proceed with strategic planning. The one they usually use they call "internally generated from on high." Microsoft is a company of leaders. It's a company of people who are there because they are smart and have good ideas. People are expected to say what should happen in their area of responsibility. The way the company culture works is if you have an idea and you are hard-driving enough, you are going to get your idea through. In this product group, product decisions were made based on an idea someone had that they had tried out on their own – "internally generated from on high". The group was looking for a different approach that involved a large group of people and allowed those people to create the strategy they were going to implement.

When the search conference was presented as an option for product planning, the reaction was something like: "I think I get it. Let's sketch it out." Then the light went on. "This is great! This is exactly what we are looking for." They liked the search conference approach because it offered a way to bring people together in a face-to-face meeting to plan and implement their own future.

The purpose statement of the search conference was: to bring together creative people from across the organization to develop and implement a plan for the most desirable future of the group's products.

They got to the part of the search conference where they started discussing the group's most desirable future. They were looking into the future and clarifying what the desirable futures could be. As they discussed possible futures for the group, conflict happened. People were disagreeing about everything.

Rationalizing conflict

When conflict arises in a search conference, we rationalize the conflict. We don't ignore it, diminish it, or placate people. Instead, we take conflict seriously. People work to understand and clarify their real differences. When people disagree we go through a process of making the conflict understandable – slowly, systematically, with the whole group, we identify the fine line between agreement and disagreement.

Rationalization of conflict means making our differences clear and understandable, and it worked like this in the search conference. We hung small group reports on the most desirable future next to each other on a wall, and reported them aloud. Two sets of questions were raised – first, questions of clarification from the groups, and then a question as to whether anybody cannot live with or is not prepared to work towards any item on any of the reports. The rule is: if we disagree on a desirable future point, it goes on the "Disagreed List." Once on the list, it ceases to be part of the further work of the group. After all, if the people in the room are critical to developing and carrying out the strategy, and even one of them clearly disagrees with a direction, we'd rather know about it sooner than later.

Chapter 9
Splitting
System
Principles at
Microsoft:
How
Rationalizing
Conflict
Turned One
System into
Two

In this process we are not assuming there will or should be consensus. To do so is unrealistic, particularly on topics where there are legitimate adversarial positions. The aim is to precisely establish common ground and to know exactly where the thin line between agreement and disagreement is located.

In this case it was the halfway point of the search conference – well into the desirable future – and the wall charts with the "Disagreed List" were loaded with stuff. But the wall charts with the agreed desirable future were tiny. As we looked at this we began to ask ourselves: Is this group actually a business unit? Is there a strategy here that these people are going to be able to get behind collectively? Are these people actually working for the same company? Is this business a system? We began to ask fundamental questions.

A dilemma – what to do?

At dinner, the general manager asked Kevin, chuckling a bit nervously: "Gee Kevin, when does the strategy part happen?" We began to realize that in terms of identifying an agreed strategy, we were in trouble. Kevin and the manager brainstormed two approaches. Approach number one was to go back into the room following dinner and say: "OK, it sounds like we are having a hard time building agreement around this strategy, so I am going to decide what to do, because we have to build a business here."

They discussed this and what might play out if it were to take place. They also discussed the fact that they had set out to do a participative process and that this approach would not be participative. So they considered the participative alternative. They were not sure, but maybe the group can figure out what to do. Even though she could not see a way through, the general manager trusted the group to come up with the right way forward.

So, following dinner, with the disagreed list mounted on the wall, the general manager said to the participants:

"OK, I'll admit it, I'm stumped. I have no idea what kind of strategy we are going to build from this. Can anybody help figure this out?"

Normally, in a search conference, disagreements that make it to the disagreed list cease to be a part of the continuing conversation of the group. The group shifts to discovering the common ground they can agree to and make their plans accordingly. But in this search, the disagreements were too fundamental. So we decided to analyze the disagreements to see what we could learn.

The group of thirty-nine began talking. Over the course of the next forty-five minutes, three themes began to emerge from the disagreed list. They thought rather than focus on what they don't agree on, perhaps there are some things on the disagreed list that they do agree on. There were three themes and each theme represented an area of agreement. It started to become clear through the discussion that these three themes could be categories people could pursue.

After more dialogue on the three themes, we decided to test the three-theme theory. Kevin said to the group: "Let's see where we all fall related to those themes in terms of our excitement and energy to pursue them as strategies." He asked people to get up and move to corners of the room identified by the themes, using the criteria of excitement and energy. Everyone moved to one of the spots in the room. As it turned out, three people ended up in one corner. The rest (eighteen and eighteen) evenly split between the other two themes.

We looked at this and said: "This is interesting. What do you think about this distribution?" They began to talk about it and people stated why they were standing in each corner, why their theme was an energizing strategy and how we could win by pursuing that direction.

The group of three talked about how they saw their strategy working. As they continued to talk, they identified that what they were saying fitted really well with what one of the larger

Chapter 9
Splitting
System
Principles at
Microsoft:
How
Rationalizing
Conflict
Turned One
System into
Two

groups was also saying. They said: "We could align ourselves around the kinds of products they are talking about." So they moved to that group. The search conference continued with two groups now working towards becoming altogether different businesses.

Two system principles not one

In open systems terms, what they discovered in the product group search conference was that they were two systems, not one. It was the open discussion and rationalization of conflict that proved the point.

Each and every system has its own unique "principle", which we call the "system principle". A system principle is a clear statement that communicates the organization's unique purpose, direction, and relationship with its environment. The desirable future and goals that emerge from the search conference contain the elements of the organization's system principle. If there isn't one, then an organization is not a system. If there is more than one system principle, two or more separate systems may exist within one organization.

What was so exciting about our experience was that it felt at first that there was no strategy, no agreement, and the top person was going to have to suck it all up to herself and drive her own strategy forward. And who knows what she would have come up with working from the top? She might not have thought of two groups with two separate products. Instead, the manager trusted the group and let the search conference work its way through the problem. The group used its disagreements constructively. By openly clarifying and understanding their fundamental differences they discovered something new. They learned that they were two systems, each needing its own strategy and purpose.

Summary

The search conference has been a valuable method for doing participative planning at Microsoft. Since 1995, there have been more than twenty search conferences resulting in clearly agreed, winning strategies. A quote from a business unit manager best characterizes the success of the search method:

> "When we finished the search, it didn't seem as if we had done anything radically different. Three months later I noticed that people had a deeper understanding of our business strategy than ever before. There were fewer questions about why we were doing the products we were doing. We were much clearer about what we agreed on."

Postscript: the three Ps – purpose, participants and pre-work

We used the usual search conference process. To us at Microsoft, a successful search conference means purpose, participants, and pre-work. We call them the "Three Ps."

Purpose Before going into the search conference we found it was critical to get all the participants together to clarify the purpose of the conference. We would wordsmith, craft, and articulate a purpose statement that all forty people could agree with. It was critical because it got everybody on board. The statement says why we are going off-site for three days. One of the other Microsoft search conferences included a 3-hour meeting to craft a purpose statement (a very long meeting by Microsoft standards) on a Tuesday, and then the following Sunday morning brought twenty-nine software developers together to begin a search. That can only be accomplished by a clear and compelling purpose.

Participants Getting the right people to the conference was critical. Our criteria were simple and straightforward: people with knowledge of the business who are willing and able to be part of the implementation of the plan. This led to selection of a "deep slice" of people up, down, and across

Chapter 9
Splitting
System
Principles at
Microsoft:
How
Rationalizing
Conflict
Turned One
System into
Two

the organization. If someone had critical knowledge of the business, but was not part of implementing the plan, we often interviewed them as part of pre-work.

Pre-work Pre-work meant having participants go out to important stakeholders – internal and external to Microsoft – before the search conference. They interviewed stakeholders to get their perspectives, expectations, and information about the market. The information was put on what we call at Microsoft a "public folder". Public folder is an intranet device that allows everyone to review the interview results before the search conference.

Reference
1 Parts of this story come from Kevin Purcell's presentation at the European Ecology of Work conference in Dublin, Ireland, in 1998. Kevin Purcell is a senior consultant for Microsoft's leadership development group. He designed and facilitated this search conference.

Chapter 10

Cooperative Water Planning: A Search Conference for the Colorado Front Range

by Robert Rehm

Search conferences are often used to bring a diverse group of people together to tackle a difficult community issue and develop a plan of action. This one is different. This is the story of how water engineers from several Colorado communities on the Front Range of the Rocky Mountains used a search conference to become a group that could do its own planning.

The story begins more than one hundred years ago, when settlers began moving west to Colorado to make their fortunes as miners. As the gold and silver mines panned out in the late 1880s, farming and ranching took over as the main industries. Settlers "civilized" the old mining towns of Denver, Colorado Springs, and Boulder. There was a belief at the time that as farmers planted crops, rain would follow somehow from the hand of God. And the railroad companies sold Colorado as the land of endless opportunity.

The "water wars", with their violence and legal maneuverings, began almost immediately that settlers realized their survival and prosperity depended entirely on access to fresh water in a semi-arid southwestern climate. They noticed quickly that rain did not come after they started planting. As Wendell Berry, the farmer philosopher, put it: settlers out West "had vision, but no sight". They knew what they wanted but did not appreciate where they were. As the region grew, experts and politicians responded to disputes by enacting complicated water laws, building a multitude of dams on the Colorado and other rivers, and treating water as a rare, private resource like the gold and silver of days gone by.

As we move the story up to the present day, we see some significant changes in Colorado culture. As the 20th century was coming to a close, hi-tech and other new industries were moving in and the tourist industry was also on the rise. Population was booming. Local political leaders and planners proposed the building of a new dam northwest of Denver on the Two Forks River, to provide plenty of fresh water into the next century for a growing and increasingly thirsty populace. This time the planners failed to appreciate the extent of change in the broader social environment, as forces combined to defeat the project. Every interest group – tourism, environmentalists, Chambers of Commerce, agriculture, new industry, and sportsmen – rose up against the dam. The final blow came from the administrative agencies in Washington who rejected the project because of the environmental impact. It was back to the drawing board for water planners.

In 1993, Colorado Governor Roy Romer, faced with more pressure to deal with imminent water crises, called together the political leaders of the Colorado Front Range communities. The Front Range region of Colorado is bounded by the Continental Divide (the peaks of the Rocky Mountains) to the west, New Mexico to the south, Wyoming to the north, and Colorado farm land to the east. The major cities are Denver, Colorado Springs, Loveland, Boulder, and Fort Collins. The governor, an avid proponent of collaboration, challenged the leaders to find new ways of cooperating across their political boundaries to plan for future water needs. He suggested they form the Front Range Water Forum. The first act of the Forum was to pull together all the key water engineers and experts from the Front Range communities into what they called the Technical Action Group (TAC). TAC's job would be to work collaboratively with hired expert water planners to develop projects for water usage that would satisfy the needs of the region well into the next century without building new dams.

The TAC's first few meetings went nowhere because of mistrust and political suspicion. Several of the TAC members had participated in a successful water quality search conference two years earlier.[1] They were members of the Colorado River Headwaters Forum, a network organization that emerged from that search conference. They suggested a search conference to bring the group together around a plan they could implement. No one could think of a better way around this stalemate and the conference happened in spring, 1994.

The participants were forty technical water engineers from the Front Range and the consulting group hired by the Forum to do the technical research required to make the plan feasible. This was truly the group responsible for carrying out cooperative water projects over the next several years. They had an intense need to find direction and get organized. Outsiders were not required and would only have detracted from their important task.

The purpose of the search conference was for this group of water engineers to develop cooperative water projects for the Front Range communities of Colorado.

The search conference funnel design looked like this:

Chapter 10
Cooperative
Water
Planning:
A Search
Conference for
the Colorado
Front Range

Changes in the world important into the future

Probable and desirable future of the Colorado Front Range

The history of Front Range water: what it means to us

Current analysis of water planning

Most desirable future of Front Range water use

Scoping cooperative projects

Organizing to complete the projects

Implementing the projects

The search conference occurred under "social island" conditions at a resort near Colorado Springs and lasted three days. It began with dinner, then a briefing spelling out the conference purpose and agenda, and a discussion of mutual expectations. Starting with "changes in the world" was particularly important for this group for two reasons. One, they needed to create water projects from the perspective of all the uncertainties in their planning environment; and two, they needed to quickly find out that they had something in common: a shared perception of the larger environment in which they were planning. During the brainstorm one of the participants who had been in the first search conference publicly remarked, "I feel it happening again. We are coming together already."

We decided to move from changes in the world directly to an analysis of the region's probable and desirable future, instead of keeping the focus on the world. We gambled that bringing the group's attention to ideals for their region would provide a meaningful background for the next day's development of the future of water usage. The ideals for the region ranged from cooperative living, to controlled development, to a beautiful natural environment, to ideals of social welfare and education. The group agreed fairly easily to these ideals and put the concept of "conservation" up on their "disagreed list" because they could not agree on what it meant. The history activity was useful as people talked about key turning points and milestones in Colorado water history. The Two Forks dam controversy, failure of litigation to solve real problems, and the advent of the Colorado River Headwaters Forum were top of the list. It was clear that considering the system's history had brought them to a new point of possibilities.

The current system analysis also converged on the need to drop old contentious ways, in favor of creating collaborative approaches. The most desirable future for water use resulted in the group quickly agreeing to four major projects for cooperating across their municipal boundaries. One of the most interesting involved drawing a public water resource map – the first time in Colorado history. Until the search conference, Front Range communities considered their water resources as secret as gold. For the group to publicly draw a map of their water resources was the realization of their shared ideals from the day before, about the future of Colorado – cooperation, controlled development, and social welfare.

After getting the project statements clear, people went into four small groups by choice to scope out the details of each project, including identifying ways around constraints. A tense moment occurred when two water engineers from communities embroiled in a water-use lawsuit found themselves in the same group. At the end of the session, the two men proudly had us take a picture of them standing together next to the chart containing their project plan.

The search conference ended with a session in which participants organized themselves into a democratic working group, with a team structure to sustain them over the next two years of project implementation.

139

Chapter 10
Cooperative
Water
Planning:
A Search
Conference for
the Colorado
Front Range

Three of the four projects were implemented. The fourth fell through because of lack of political support at the local level. This prospect was predicted during the session on constraints. Everyone knew this was a high-risk item, but decided to give it a try anyway. Fortunately, the search conference is designed not to put all the strategy "eggs" in one basket.

Eight years later, the Front Range continues to grow and prosper – one of the fastest growing parts of the country. Water is still a challenging issue, but communities are dealing with it more openly and cooperatively than ever before. And no dams have been built or even proposed in the years since the search conference. The Front Range search conference was a watershed, so to speak, moving communities from "water wars" to collaborative problem-solving.

Reference
1   To read about the first water search conference see: Bob Rehm, Elaine Granata, and Rita Schweitz: "Water Quality in the Upper Colorado River Basin," in Marvin Weisbord, *Discovering Common Ground*, Berrett-Koehler Publishers, Inc., San Francisco, 1992. Bob Rehm, Elaine Granata, and Rita Schweitz designed and facilitated this first water search conference as well as the Front Range conference discussed in this chapter.

Chapter 11

The Madison Benefits Group Story: The Search Conference Meets The Hoop and The Tree

by Evangeline Caridas and Nancy Cebula

This chapter tells the story of how a small benefits company involved all its workers in a search conference to find ways to manage fast growth. The authors go beyond just telling the story. They introduce us to a model of ecological health useful for any organization. They show us how the model called the "Hoop and the Tree", played out in this search conference.

Part One: The Hoop and The Tree

In his groundbreaking book *The Hoop and the Tree*, Chris Hoffman describes how organizations are in balance when they have both the Hoop and Tree fulfilled.[1] The Hoop represents relationship, interconnectedness, and the feminine. The Tree signifies aspiration, achievement, and the masculine. Within each person, each organization, each culture, both feminine and masculine dimensions can be found, to one degree or another.

In Chris Hoffman's words:

Imagine a vertical axis running through the center of your being, from deep in the ground up to your highest aspiration . . . Recall a time when you felt especially grounded or rooted. Think of your highest aspiration and what it feels like to be stretching toward that goal. This is the Tree, which roots you, centers you, and offers you a way to ascend to the light of your highest aspiration, and a way to be fruitful. Imagine also the Tree encircled by a Hoop on a horizontal plane, with the center of the Hoop pierced by the trunk of the Tree. Remember your family or some other group that encircles you with love. Recall being surrounded by the beauty of nature. The Hoop brings you into relationship with the rest of the universe. Together the Hoop-and-Tree image is a pattern or model for wholeness in the universe.

We've used the search conference as a method for designing and implementing successful change for many years. We have always thought of search conferences as producing two big outcomes: a detailed action plan AND a strong and energetic community that is fully committed to implementing that plan. But it wasn't until reading this book that we saw how it also creates the opportunity to perfectly balance the masculine, aspiration (what we want to be – the plan) and the feminine, relationship (how we can work together, resolve differences, learn about each other – the community). So we can now describe the search conference as a unique process that integrates and balances the Hoop and the Tree within the organizational or community setting.

In organizations that are more masculine or achievement-oriented, a search conference allows people to spend time focusing on relationship, on the feminine dimension. An organization that is more relationship-based or more feminine will find that the search conference allows people to home in on the search for ideals, developing visions of the future, and detailed action plans to make those visions a reality.

Each step in a search conference is designed to bring this balance to the activity. The explicit focus is the task, but there is a huge implicit focus on relationship-building. The search conference begins literally with the Hoop, where people introduce themselves in small circles, or in a large circle, depending on the size of the group. Throughout the search, people move in and out of different small groups so that everyone will have a chance to work with everyone else. Although this isn't discussed, it provides the environment where a strong network of relationships can develop and become the planning community.

The second activity, about changes in the world, is more achievement-oriented: "Let's take a look at what has been happening, what has been changing in the last 5-7 years." The group sits in a semi-circle, facing the chart paper, as they talk about their experience of the environment. The analysis that follows is also geared more to aspiration and achievement. Yet people work in small groups, circled around their chart paper, relating to one another.

The history session involves all the participants sitting in a large circle, telling stories of milestones, events, achievements, activities, and important occurrences from the system's past. Sometimes people begin to talk about the history of their relationships with key players and with each other. This is the most Hoop-like activity in a search conference. However, appreciating the system's history also uncovers things about the past that are deeply rooted (Tree) and valuable for the future.

The desirable future phase of the search conference is very Tree-oriented – "What do we want our future to look like?" But the style of working is, again, very Hoop-like. People sit in small circles around a chart, with conversation moving all around, with everyone taking part in the brainstorming and in the decision-making, as they develop an agreed product for their group.

Following this, the outputs from each group are integrated into a common ground agenda for action-planning, The

Chapter 11
The Madison
Benefits
Group Story:
The Search
Conference
Meets The
Hoop and
The Tree

content under discussion is aspiration but the style of working – with all participants again in a large circle, able to see each other and all of the chart paper, and come to agreement on their vision for the most desirable future of their system – is feminine. Again the balance of the Hoop and the Tree is fulfilled.

The final action-planning phase also brings the Hoop and the Tree together as it discusses in detail what needs to be done and how it will get done. People aspire and set goals and how to measure them. Relationship is built into each action plan with discussions of who needs to be involved and how we need to be organized to get our plan accomplished. Often after a search conference, people comment that they now "deal with people differently". Not only are they working on action steps and goals together, they do so within an enhanced circle of relationships – the Hoop and the Tree in balance.

The following story is an example of how a small, growing organization used the search conference to bring people together to plan for their future and, as part of the process, bring relationship and aspiration into harmony.

Part Two: Madison Benefits Group – Growing Pains Soothed by a Search Conference

Every entrepreneurial company experiences growing pains. Madison Benefits Group (MBG) is a boutique company that provides benefits administration for medium-sized companies that want to outsource this aspect of employee benefits. They specialize in creating customized health, dental, life, and long-term care insurance packages and other benefits to fit the needs of each client. MBG is staffed by long-term career employees. A surge in clients in this competitive industry meant Madison Benefits had to grow, and fast.

New employees were hired as needed, but there was no system for integrating them. New clients signed up in droves, but there was no system for controlling work volume. Employees of Madison Benefits were challenged and thrilled with their company's success, but struggled to meet demands that quickly got out of hand. Madison Benefits consistently delivered high-quality, measurable results. As a result, clients continued to flock. But projects were often finalized at the expense of a positive work environment. The workplace was pressured, and employees often stayed late at night to finish their commitments with the exceptional skill, attention, and professionalism demanded by Madison Benefit's reputation.

The partners were concerned that traditional strategic planning would not address their needs. As one partner said, "We need to have goals, but we also need to recognize that the business is too volatile to follow a strict plan." President and founder Beth Madison sought a means of taming her company's surging growth, and contacted Caridas Consulting Group, where she heard about the search conference. A decision was made to use this methodology to help the strained company develop a systematic and adaptive approach to growth, without losing the strong relationships already developed.

Consultants and company leadership met to assess the pressing business and organizational issues facing the company. These meetings helped to refine the search conference purpose and identify key people whose input would be necessary to the success of the planning process. A decision was made to include all employees and managers in the search conference.

The search conference occurred over the course of several days. The meeting took participants through discussions of the external business environment, the workplace environment, and company history, and eventually led them to a point of decision and action. The search conference helped people identify the core of Madison's strengths, such as respect for the company's leadership and hard-working employees, and use them to formulate solutions to problems.

Creating a community and the systems to keep it running

Chapter 11
The Madison
Benefits
Group Story:
The Search
Conference
Meets The
Hoop and
The Tree

smoothly, proved to be the firm's most urgent goals. Without systems and a community in place, people had no method for anticipating the costs, resources, and time required by each project. This recurrent problem was eating away at the profit margin. While this was a concern for everyone, many employees were not shown how they could help boost the profit margin. Poor communication among teams further compromised company systemization.

The very process of the search conference helped the company move toward solutions. It brought together people who did not always see each other, so that, according to one employee, "People who don't normally have access to each other really bonded." Improving communications was already a major goal, and the search conference initiated this. "It opened people's eyes and our communication channels," remarked one employee. It also provided a forum in which individual employees discussed their careers as related to Madison Benefits Group. The participation of company founder, Beth Madison, gave all employees valuable and unique knowledge of the company's history, and from that, they derived a sense of belonging and ownership.

As one manager said, "One goal is for people to feel good going the extra mile, not because they have to, but because they want to." Ownership of their work and commitment to the company motivated employees to go that extra mile. To help themselves accomplish this, they developed systems based on their collected knowledge, work experience, and most successful practices. From this they generated guidelines to help employees estimate project costs realistically. This structured approach enabled the necessary growth in profit margin. People are more likely to follow through on plans they create themselves, and Madison employees left the search conference eager to get started.

The search conference laid the groundwork for a new working environment, generated ideas for improvement, and sent employees out the door with an action plan already underway. The experience taught them how to work in small teams, building on each other's knowledge, to adapt Madison Benefits and stay at the top of a changing, competitive market. As a partner said, "MBG is a known force in the market place." The search conference gave Madison Benefits the tools to keep their reputation for excellence during a period of tremendous growth, and to continue to build on the strong relationships that existed between managers, employees, and customers.

Part Three: The Hoop and The Tree within Madison Benefits Group

With the preceding story in mind, let's apply the Hoop and Tree to the Madison Benefits Group and its search conference. Most private sector organizations are Tree organizations, built on aspiration and achievement, not necessarily relationship. One of the unique and intriguing things about this story is hidden between the lines. Madison Benefits Group is a Hoop company, one built on relationship. As the search conference proceeded, it became apparent that part of the growing pains experienced by MBG were due to the introduction of more (formal) Tree elements into the company. As more business appeared, there was a need for more people to join the company. Systems and processes designed for a very small company where people knew each other really well became strained. Due to the speed of change, people were recruited, but not getting the time to integrate into the company. The explosion of new work created a "get the work done whatever it takes" attitude. People who had been there for a while felt a bit marginalized and new people did not have time to get to know how things had been done. Communication systems that had worked well in the past were no longer able to keep people informed and in touch with each other.

In this case, the search conference became a means of integrating Hoop relationships that had served MBG well in

Chapter 11
The Madison
Benefits
Group Story:
The Search
Conference
Meets The
Hoop and
The Tree

the past with Tree elements, such as the more formal operational and structural systems that were being introduced to create and achieve sustainable growth.

The search conference was the first time that *all* the employees of Madison Benefits Group came together face to face since the new staff had come on board. Even the part-time, college-student administrative assistants were invited to participate. This decision to include everyone was a key element in the success of transition from a mostly Hoop organization to one where Hoop and Tree are balanced and integrated.

The activities in this search conference played out pretty much as expected – with one notable difference. The history session was unique. In the Madison Benefits Group story, the history session consisted almost entirely of stories of various participants' relationships with the founder of the company, Beth Madison. Generally in history sessions, people tell a few stories of relationship. However, they are usually interspersed with stories of events and milestones. This history session gave people a chance to hear others' connection to Beth Madison, and painted a picture of an organization founded on relationship. Several of the new people told how they had met Beth Madison years ago and were eventually able to join her company. Other new people spoke of their briefer relationships. At the end of this session, various milestones were briefly noted, to give new people a sense of what had gone on before they joined the company. However, the emphasis was clearly on relationships with the founder.

It also became clear that, as the company grew, there was not enough time in the day for everyone to be as closely related to Beth Madison. Various desirable future scenarios described what MBG could look like with relationship still a core value of the company, but with people building relationships with each other and working together to achieve sustainable growth and accomplishments.

In the action-planning, details emerged as to how people would implement this new way of working together. They worked out ways of involving more people in setting goals within their work teams and for the entire company, rebuilding relationships within their work teams, developing effective communications processes and building relationships across team boundaries – throughout the whole organization. They initiated plans to help each individual see their part in serving customers, achieving goals, and in the success of the company as a whole. The discussion of the link between company performance and employee rewards began in the search conference. A new reward system was implemented later to the mutual satisfaction and benefit.

During follow-up conversations, people reported that they felt that they were working together better, that information was communicated clearly and in a more timely manner. "We are working smarter; we don't have to stay late so many days every week." People still enjoyed their relationship with Beth Madison, and were building relationships with other managers and employees. There were new customers coming in regularly and 'old' customers reported that the level of service was what they expected from MBG. The leadership team was beginning to explore ways to continue to grow in a sustainable manner and to create more responsibility and decision-making opportunities for each employee.

In our experience, traditional processes usually yield traditional results. Organizations of all kinds are strewn with strategic plans that have gone nowhere, sitting on bookshelves gathering dust, because people were not involved in the planning process. If you want your organization to achieve its desirable future, building community along the way, use a process designed to harmonize the Hoop of relationship and the Tree of aspiration – the search conference.

Chapter 11
The Madison
Benefits
Group Story:
The Search
Conference
Meets The
Hoop and
The Tree

Reference
[1] Hoffman, Chris. *The Hoop and the Tree: A Compass for Finding a Deeper Relationship with All Life*. San Francisco: Council Oak Books, 2000.

Chapter 12

Creating Alignment in a Major Project: The Search Conference in Another Guise

by Graham Benjamin

This is not a search conference story; it is about how, with ingenuity, you can apply search conference principles to just about any kind of planning meeting – the search conference in another guise. This story reveals how the principles of a search conference can be used to create the partnership and alignment essential to on-time, on-budget and safe delivery across a number of globally dispersed players.

The principles of the search conference can be usefully applied in many ways and contexts. This account explains an application intended to produce alignment at senior level between contract holders in a major international construction project. The project task was to design, develop, build and install an oil and gas field offshore West Africa with a total value of around one billion US dollars. The facilities under construction included a large number of wells and associated platforms and pipelines plus a floating storage and production facility of super-tanker size, in itself of world-class proportions and complexity. Alignment embraced several dimensions, notably:

Morning — EGOSS *Product, serv*
afternoon — Components & Services *culture*
individuals

♦ Five main contract parties: the client and four consortia of contractor companies
♦ Different professional groups, from reservoir engineers to drillers to construction engineers to operators and all the supporting functions
♦ A variety of cultures: national, religious, linguistic, corporate
♦ Geographical spread by time zone and location, from Korea through the Middle East, Europe, from USA to Africa.

Design Principles

These are faithful to the basis for the search conference. They are:

♦ Stakeholder involvement bringing all pieces of the puzzle together
♦ Self-managed discovery, dialogue, learning and planning
♦ Representing and exploring the whole open system
♦ Focus on the work
♦ Acknowledging, exploring, resolving or agreeing to disagree about any areas of genuine conflict related to the agreed work task but placing emphasis and energy on enlarging the common ground

Summarized as:

Right task + Right people + Right setting
=
Unprecedented agreement about and energy for action

The Alignment Task

The task was to support the client project manager in addressing the complexity of the project's contract structure and organization. The challenge was to design a process of engagement, efficient in time, space and financing that would nonetheless embrace difficult issues in real time. Each of the contract areas had interface needs one of another which would affect the capacity of each area to perform and, if left unacknowledged, would be likely to disturb the project's critical path of activity and dramatically reduce the chances of success.

Background

The project was well advanced when we started this piece of work. All the initial tests for viability had been completed and conceptual designs had been agreed. Invitations to tender had been completed and contractor consortia had been selected. The client was ready to commit to contracts. Thus far all negotiations had been discrete, the client working one-to-one with each contract area. Now the "one project" concept had to be addressed for the first time to produce alignment across the whole venture, which in the fabrication and construction phase would be dispersed worldwide. Final installation and commissioning would see convergence of all facilities and equipment to the operating area offshore West Africa in about two years' time. The government, through their ministry and the regulator, were key stakeholders and were participants in the process.

Divergence-Convergence

The design used a classic "divergence-convergence" approach, just like search. Quite simply this entails firstly the opening up of participation – the divergence – to embrace more or all of the subject and people. Secondly the convergence stage narrows the subject and the people involved towards an agreed

153

Chapter 12
Creating
Alignment in a
Major Project:
The Search
Conference in
Another Guise

outcome. This basic two-stage process has been found to be successful in satisfying two of the design principles of the search conference: stakeholder involvement and representing and exploring the whole system.

For the case in question, participants were globally dispersed. It would not be efficient or possible to bring them together more than once or for very long. Yet preparatory work had to be done to ensure that the bringing together would be on a basis of understanding likely to encourage convergence.

The work started with the client management team, (step one below). It diverged from there to include all the main contract management teams (step two), and to give them time to consult in turn with their principal sub-contractors, where necessary. Questions for clarification and suggestions for changes moved back and forth through the client management team during this period, (step three). Finally (step four) it was time to converge, literally and metaphorically, in one room on one day to search for the agreements and relationships necessary to weld a globally dispersed enterprise into one team.

So How Did it Work? A Four-step Process

Step one: Creating the initial focus (or, making the point from which to diverge)

The client project manager decided to appoint a third party to facilitate the process, someone not identified through direct employment with any of the participants. He chose an external consultant in organization development, a freelancer, with whom he had worked before and therefore with known experience of this kind of process.

The consultant met with the client project manager and his team to help create a common sense between them of the challenge and to consider options for design of the process. This team in itself embraced several nationalities and disciplines and was by no means convergent in its thinking.

Over two short sessions and a whole day workshop two key outputs were produced: agreement on the "divergent-convergent" process design and a set of "project execution principles". These were intended as an attitudinal and behavioral proposal for how the process and the project could be aligned and conducted. They developed and added definition to the project vision, mission (or core purpose) and team values statements. These became recognized as useful themes around which alignment could begin.

The key statements were:

Chapter 12
Creating
Alignment in a
Major Project:
The Search
Conference in
Another Guise

Vision: "To be recognized for delivering a project that is acknowledged for safe, profitable development and operation of shallow water oil fields, thus establishing [the client's] offshore project realization capability." Note the values expressed in this statement and the order in which they occur. These were considered to be non-negotiable by participants.

Mission: "The development of the [name] field within project schedule and budget, realizing steady-state operational targets before hand-over to the asset manager, to meet the expectations of the joint venture partners and other stakeholders." The mission was considered to be the client's prerogative and as such was communicated and consulted for clarity but not for content.

Team values:
♦ Awareness / clear object / common goals
♦ Communication
♦ Openness / honesty / confidence
♦ Understanding capabilities / balance of skills
♦ "We" not "I" / collective responsibilities / no blame culture / share success and failure
♦ Trust / empowerment / acceptance of responsibilities *[acceptance of weaknesses or lack of experience]*
♦ Recognition of diversity

These values were explicitly intended as guidelines to start a process of consultation carried out during step two and some changes were made in consequence.

Project Execution Principles:
A two-page document of eleven principles, crafted by the client management team formed the key part of communication and consultation during the divergent phase, (steps two and three). It successfully created discussion, disagreement and clarification and was significantly amended as a result of this process. It became the prime vehicle for convergence and was signed in its final and agreed form by all main contract parties during step four. The eleven points covered the detail of how agreed key features for project success would be achieved. These are some of the items featured:

♦ A culture of openness, professionalism and team spirit
♦ Focus on vital objectives (safety, environmental impact, plant integrity, cost and schedule)
♦ Minimize delays
♦ Apply the agreed "no change" policy
♦ Client working relationship to contractor (detail and style of involvement in work on-site)
♦ Share lessons learned / apply best practice
♦ The contract to be used as a reference document and managed according to these principles

Step two: Divergence, or getting buy-in from major stakeholders
The consultant traveled to the project managers of each of the contractor consortia. Introductions had been made by the client project manager in a previous conversation. The consultant had sessions with the leadership of each consortium that ranged across the contract areas from several meetings to full workshops. Typically, the consortia addressed first their own statements, this being a meeting of the consortia

companies' objectives and aspirations. Then they compared these positions with their contract situation and the overall project mission, team values and execution principles. Reconciliation was effected internally within the consortium and for the project overall where possible. Remaining issues of interpretation and difference at the whole-project level were highlighted. A dialogue was created between the client project management team and the main contract teams in step three.

Contractor offices were remote from each other, in The Netherlands, UK, France, and Monaco. Later in the project they were remoter still – Korea, Dubai, Singapore, West Africa – which fully justified the effort made in this process to create alignment based on principle and to build relationships through real work together.

Step three: Divergence and the start of convergence, or agreed overall approach

The client project manager monitored with his team the progress across the contractor consortia and worked, through the client team representatives in the contractor offices, to resolve matters of interpretation and issues where possible. Simultaneously the design for convergence and alignment (step four) was evolving, also informed by the progress with the consortia. This design was tested with prospective participants whilst it was being developed. The proposed project vision, mission, and team values proved robust throughout this step. Detailed changes to the project execution principles were proposed by contractor consortia and accepted.

Each of the principles of the search conference had now been addressed, but not sufficiently:

♦ *Stakeholder involvement* had been tested for appropriateness and then used to develop the process, but only on a one-to-one engagement basis with the client. Now that agreement had been reached on the fundamentals, it was time to bring all the elements of the project into one room.

157

Chapter 12
Creating
Alignment in a
Major Project:
The Search
Conference in
Another Guise

- *Self-managed discovery and learning.* The client system had been facilitated remotely to engage in a process of consultation to create the conditions for convergence. This had involved revealing, exploring (and in some instances reconciling) differences, by learning from and about each other.
- *Representing and exploring the whole system* had occurred remotely in step three but was to have its full and most active expression in step four (below).
- *Focus on the work.* The project execution principles acted as the main vehicle for this with an explicitly designed and consulted process (steps one to four) which was transparent in its design and content to all participants.
- *Dealing with conflict firmly rooted in the reality of the agreed work task.* The work task must be explicit. The proposals from step one provided that. Trust must be created. The explicit and transparent process did that. This is the whole point behind the divergent part of the process. It is not only to find out who the best people are for the search. It is also to create general confidence that the search will be properly conducted with a reasonable chance of a successful outcome which all participants can and will commit to.
- *Emphasis on common ground.* This was the whole point of this particular process.

Now the expensive step could be undertaken to have people travel the world to meet together.

Step four: Convergence, or conduct workshop

The workshop was designed to accommodate all the senior managers and leaders from across the project, some fifty in all. This number embraced the most significant people involved in the first three steps, defined as contract holders or managers with key interface responsibilities between contract areas. (Consortia managers had taken the opportunity to involve more of their people in step two). In all, some thirteen stakeholder entities were represented, focused into five main groups: the client and the four main contract areas.

With a two-day design spread across three calendar days that embraced social and team-building activities, the workshop essentially focused first on sessions designed to highlight and resolve differences to a common set of execution principles. Secondly, and only when the first had been completed, opportunity was created for consortia to meet in live session to address issues related to common execution needs. Third and last, a "market place" was created in the ballroom used as the workshop's main space, whereby work issues were identified one to another across the consortia interfaces in a controlled sequence of problem identification and resolution. This last feature ensured that maximum advantage was derived from, first, the convergence produced around agreement on the project execution principles and second, having the key people all together in one place at the same time!

The workshop design itself used the divergence-convergence model, with a common starting point. The starting point was at 1500 hours on the first day. Participants were greeted by the client project manager and a shared social experience. A troupe of professional theatre musicians worked with participants in mixed groups. The groups practiced with percussion instruments to produce a short performance, presented in turn to the rest of the workshop. This was a lively and hugely enjoyable experience even for the most hesitant, contained as it was by the musicians within a relatively 'safe' experiential framework. Many of the participants had not met each other before and certainly not face-to-face. None had all been in one room together all at the same time. This event took three hours and formed a good "here and now" shared social experience which actually and symbolically created the spirit of openness and exploration required by the project principles and the event itself. Dinner followed and the evening closed with a short address from the client project manager and the

Chapter 12
Creating
Alignment in a
Major Project:
The Search
Conference in
Another Guise

consultant, who spoke about the design of the workshop: purpose, objectives and program.

Next morning, "day two", divergence began. Working in the ballroom of the hotel where the workshop was located (so that accommodation and work areas were all commonly and easily situated) each of the five main project areas had brought displays that visually communicated their work and work plan for the project. We did not want to take for granted that all areas of the project had equal or sufficient knowledge of the other (there were work disciplines represented who did not necessarily work closely together) and it was necessary to stimulate thought about needs and inter-dependencies across organizational interfaces which might not yet have been identified. With a representative stationed at each display ready to explain and to answer questions, all other participants were tasked to visit in their "home" groups each of the four other display areas in a timed sequence around the room.

Mid-morning saw each of the five areas confer within their team to (a) produce adjustments to their already prepared interface issues, (b) finalize their presentation on key milestones and dependencies and (c) express any final challenges to the project execution principles.

By late morning we were ready to converge, in plenary, to work through the remaining challenges, which were now only a few, and the principles in fine detail, and to have a brief signing ceremony!

After lunch and again in plenary, convergence occurred once more as each of the five area teams presented their work plan expressed as key milestones, with their definition of the main interdependencies and interface issues, updated where appropriate by the morning session. To better manage time with the number of people involved, only questions for clarification were taken in this plenary session. A follow-up session in the work groups gave time for teams to confer together to finalize where unresolved issues existed, and to plan across the interfaces between the contract areas. This took the workshop close to the end of "day two". Before a final review of the day some lighter relief was introduced with a design competition for the "one team" project logo. Dinner was followed by informal work on the logos with submission before bedtime for judging overnight!

"Day three" opened informally with the results of the logo competition (to much amusement for some and chagrin for others) and formally with "overnight thoughts" about our progress, and how well we were conducting ourselves viewed against the principles. With a few consequential adjustments to the agenda for the rest of the day, the work recommenced in earnest.

It was time for an exercise called "the market place". Whilst the activities on "day two" were about sharing essential information, the market place exercise was where the transactions really took place. The "day two" exercises were about listening and understanding; the market place was where the deals were done for the future of the project.

To begin the market place exercise, each of the five main groups sat in their display areas in final preparation for a timed sequence of visits to each other. First "ambassadors" were briefed by their team to visit each of the other four. Some colleagues had to remain "at home" of course, to receive ambassadors from the other groups. The task was to communicate issues simply and clearly and to hear any points of clarification that should be dealt with. The task was not to resolve the issues, at this stage.

Visits took place. Then ambassadors returned and the work groups conferred among themselves. The task was for each group first to identify those issues where resolution might be possible in the next sequence. And then, more importantly and practically, to formulate clear proposals for how, when and by what means the issues would be resolved (assuming that the workshop in itself might not contain the time, people, or other means for effective resolution.) A further visit sequence then occurred to complete the market place exercise. A plenary

Chapter 12
Creating
Alignment in a
Major Project:
The Search
Conference in
Another Guise

session then took place to deal with a few issues that had been tabled which had been identified as requiring whole project attention.

A thorough workshop review followed, in plenary. The workshop objectives were tested against a post-workshop action list. Then, during a live timeline session, the next few weeks were mapped and agreed with participants. This very actively drew participants together around the immediate practical future, producing a convergence satisfying to a bunch of predominantly practical engineers. A final lessons-learned review, conducted by the client project manager as host, produced a good sense of the value of this session, by no means a foregone conclusion with this group of participants. Some practical and shared ideas for maintaining project identity and integrity also emerged. The workshop closed on schedule at 14.30.

Commentary

The whole process attempted to implement search principles in another guise, a participative event based on the search conference. Within the process, the individual workshop designs reflected the same principles, using divergence to produce convergence. In particular, the final workshop, step four, gathered the "community" within one space, in an agreed and representative way such that the real work could be completed together, all the necessary preparation having been done. Thus data-gathering, data analysis and decision-making were all completed with the whole community in real time. The process design was open and transparent. Real learning took place during the process, in that positions and definitions were modified or even changed, both by the client and other participants.

Whilst it is notoriously difficult to prove the effectiveness of such socio-technical interventions, the anecdotal belief of those in the project is that the intervention formed the foundation of project execution in relational, attitudinal and behavioral terms. Put simply, spending the time together enabled the formation of a network of relationships and a community formed around the common ground for action. This put the humanity and meaning into the contractual and organizational interfaces. It set the tone for "how we are going to do things round here", given that the doing was across wide time-zone and geographical differences. It gave identity to a widely dispersed project, enabling the various contract managers to represent the project with confidence to their head offices, thereby reducing the potential for conflict across differing corporate needs. A framework of mutual respect and understanding was created within which flexibility and conflict could be effectively managed.

The perspective proposed in this case study is that the convergence achieved did not happen by accident. Clear design principles, as established for the search conference, have proven applicable to other applications. Large-group processes in particular require careful management to succeed and principles openly and transparently applied.

The project is, at the time of writing, moving towards completion, on time, on budget and with a good safety record. It has gained the interest and respect of others in the industry.

Chapter 12
Creating Alignment in a Major Project: The Search Conference in Another Guise

Chapter 13

The Future of the YMCA of Palestine

by Steve Hobbs

Here we see how search conferencing has been used for organizational renewal and transformation in one of the most challenging environments on earth. The Palestinian YMCA brought together both internal and external stakeholders over the course of several months to re-envision and plan for its future during super-turbulent times. It's a story of hope and courage.

August 2001. We are gathered in the East Jerusalem YMCA. Outside there is turmoil. For almost one year, the Intifada – the popular uprising of the Palestinian people for basic rights – has been underway. It is a time of deep emotional, psychological, physical, and economic stress for the Palestinian community – blockades, military checkpoints, fierce gun battles, assassinations, and suicide bombers.

In the midst of this, for three days, some 60 representatives of the board of directors, managers, field and support staff, from across all levels of the YMCA organization, have gathered. They have come from the YMCAs in East Jerusalem, Bethlehem, Jericho, Ramallah, Hebron, Nablus, and Jenin. At stake is the future of the YMCA in Palestine, the largest and most reputable youth NGO in the West Bank and Gaza. This meeting is a critical point in a long and thorough process of transformation. We are gathered to consolidate a shared vision and plan for the YMCA. Much has already happened to make this meeting possible and there is much still to be done.

Despite the external turmoil and violence, the psychological and economic stress that is being faced every day, the injured, the displaced, the sleepless nights, the rattle of tanks, the helicopters overhead, there is an air of anticipation, energy, creativity and commitment to build a plan that will enable the YMCA to support and develop the young people of a future Palestine.

We are sitting in a double circle. On the walls of the large hall of the East Jerusalem YMCA, in the foyer and entrance hall, are over 180 flipchart pieces put together in colorful and lively display from the many preparatory meetings conducted over the past few months. Most of the displays are in Arabic, a few in English. National flags intersperse the displays. The people and friends of the YMCA have been hard at work thinking about their world, their past, their dreams, and plans for the future. It has been a journey of some six months over the roughest of terrains.

The Context

The World Alliance of YMCAs, with their office in Geneva, together with the International Partners of the East Jerusalem (Palestinian) YMCA, in partnership with the YMCA leadership in Jerusalem, sponsored an institutional review and re-envisioning process that came to be known as the RRE process, and that's the shorthand we'll use here.

One of the primary specifications for the process is that it should be inclusive and participatory. It should also contribute directly to building a new ethos and culture for the YMCA, as it seeks to realign and position itself for a significant role amongst young people in Palestine. RGA Consulting from

South Africa was given the work to co-design and co-facilitate the RRE process.[1] This partly came about because of my personal long-standing involvement as a volunteer in the YMCA in South Africa, Africa, and at a world level.

The Task

The central task of the RRE process was: to jointly and participatively create a shared vision for the Palestinian YMCA, a shared scorecard (goals, measures, timeframes), and a shared plan that we will implement together.

Subsidiary tasks and elements of the RRE process were:

♦ To realign and reposition the YMCA for future challenges.
♦ To prepare leadership for the future challenges and their role in leading the organization.
♦ To begin to build a new culture and ethos for the organization, that is open, participatory, and adaptive.
♦ To build capacity amongst a cadre of internal facilitators who can help support the process and assist it in becoming a way of life.
♦ Other elements of the RRE process are to give direction to issues, such as a constitution, future structure, funding, and partnerships and programme priorities.

Search Conferencing and the Design of the Project

RGA Consulting in South Africa has, through the work of and in relationship with Bob Rehm and Nancy Cebula, and the original works and writings of Fred and Merrelyn Emery, been wedded to the principles, processes, and practices of search conferencing. Since 1995, search conferencing has been central to the large-scale, whole system organizational transformation and renewal work of RGA. We have applied search conferencing widely in the South African context, in Africa, Sri Lanka, Australia, England, and now in the West Bank and Gaza.

The specific design of the RRE process included the following components or streams:

Workstream 1 – a leadership search process that involved:

♦ A personal leadership visioning with two senior directors
♦ A visioning and alignment process with the board of management (non-executives)
♦ A visioning and alignment process with the senior management team, including all the programme directors
♦ A visioning and alignment process for middle managers from across all YMCAs in the West Bank

The leadership search process involves assisting the leader group to initiate and get ahead of the organization and process. In so doing, the intention is to affirm the "leader-led" principle of organizational renewal and transformation. Central to this is preparing the leaders for the leadership challenges of the process of organizational change by giving them time and space to think together. The leaders themselves also prepare their input to the consolidation conference – their vision and dreams for the organization.

The search conference methodology of looking outward, looking backward, looking inward, and looking forward is central to this entire workstream. The process at this level ends with the leadership's vision and some provisional scorecarding. No planning is done. That is held over for the consolidation conference.

Workstream 2 – an external stakeholder process that involved gathering data and perceptions from stakeholders and feeding the information into the RRE:

♦ Five half-day workshops (search based) with a range of external stakeholders.

♦ An open-ended survey that went to all international friends and partners of the YMCA.

The stakeholder workshops can take on many forms. On average, they consist of 10 to 15 participants, often from a similar stakeholder cluster. Examples of a stakeholder cluster are: donors, suppliers, customers, and service providers. These workshops are largely focused on gathering feedback, insights, expectations and perceptions of external stakeholders. The data that is gathered is fed into the consolidation conference to enrich the process of searching. The stakeholder consultation workshops and the survey were designed within the framework of the search funnel (see chapter 2). In order to look backward (the history of the system), stories, experiences, and perceptions of the past were gathered and captured.

Representatives from each of these stakeholder consultation workshops captured all of the contributions, creatively wrote them on to flipcharts and brought them to the consolidation conference.

Workstream 3 – an internal stakeholder visioning process:

♦ Four visioning and alignment searches run in series, drawing on staff and middle and senior managers from across YMCAs.

♦ A specific search workshop for staff and managers in Gaza who were unable to travel to Jerusalem or elsewhere in the West Bank.

There were approximately 25 participants in each of these search conferences. Again the classical search funnel was the basis of these events – together searching outward, searching backward, searching inward, and searching forward. The conferences were times of significant community building across lines and divisions within the organization. Each of the search communities agreed on +/- 10 participants to carry their vision inputs forward to the forthcoming consolidation conference.

Workstream 4 – a shared vision and planning consolidation conference held over three days in Jerusalem in August 2000:

♦ Representative participants from all of the workshop events and processes held over the prior months.
♦ Two international representatives.
♦ All the outputs from other workshops colorfully and creatively displayed on wall charts, often embellished with flags, symbols, and other creative ideas.

The agreed outputs of this consolidation conference were:

♦ A shared vision
♦ A shared three-year word picture of our vision with specific goals, measures, and time frames
♦ A shared plan we will implement.

This consolidation conference was conducted in Arabic, facilitated by the internal YMCA facilitators supported by an RGA facilitator.

Workstream 5 – internal facilitator capacity-building:

♦ Developing and training eight YMCA staff and managers in the search process and in the specific RGA methodology and application.
♦ The internal YMCA facilitators conducted all of the workshops (external and internal stakeholder) other than the leadership "search" process in workstream 1.

The purpose of working with and through internal facilitators is to build higher levels of ownership, self-management, and sustainability into the process of organizational renewal and transformation. This facilitating resource team works closely with the leader group and the RGA facilitator. They are exposed to the underlying theory, roots, values, and practice of the methodology.

Workstream 6 – leadership support and capacity-building:

♦ A parallel series of team growth and development workshops for the senior management team to assist them in their collective leadership of the "new" organization. This included aspects of team visioning and scorecarding.
♦ A series of team-to-team interface sessions between the board and the senior management team to deal with obstacles, challenges, and the new leadership role going forward.

RGA Consulting has developed a leadership and team "toolbox" to assist leadership teams and work teams at all levels, to support them in their transition and in implementing the organization's strategic intent and vision in their part of the organization. The primary purpose is to enable and encourage the internalization of the shared vision of the organization within the domain of the work group and their work.

The Consolidation Conference

This was an amazing and landmark event for the YMCA in Palestine. Almost 50% of the staff was present, most managers, and a good spread of board members. It was a time of dialogue, soul searching, searching for common ground, hard work, and lots and lots of good humor and fun.

The presentations from all the earlier workshops and the survey – all in public display for the duration of the conference

– created a strong sense of "many of us having walked, and are walking this road together". It also created a sense of responsibility to those who were not present and on whose behalf we were undertaking the consolidating and planning phase. The consolidation conference combines and integrates the workstreams; and more important in some ways than the content is the coming together of the people, the hearts and minds of the organization.

The design of the consolidation conference is again largely informed by the search funnel and method, though with some specific variations and emphasis.

Time and space is provided at the beginning of the conference for bonding and allowing a new community to emerge. This is not rushed.

The looking and searching outward (environmental scan) is largely a consolidating exercise. Participants review all the outputs from the workstreams. Presentations are discouraged, dialogue and discussion are encouraged. The search community then, working in groups, constructs the shared and agreed environmental scan, drawn directly from pre-work. New insights are also captured.

The looking and searching backward looks at both the history of the system and storytelling about the process (the journey that got us together in this room). This last is central to community building and creating a strong sense of having walked, worked, and struggled together and toward a common intent. Lessons and learnings from our history are consolidated from the workstreams through community dialogue and then group work.

The keep, drop, and creates from all of the pre-work are reviewed by the participants. Perceptions, experiences, and stories are shared. Insights and themes are drawn by a group that self-organizes around this task.

The looking and searching forward (the desirable future and vision for the system) is done in a series of community and small-group interactions. Like other steps, it is drawn directly from what is in public display on the flipcharts from all the pre-work.

Synthesizing happens through the dialogue as the desirable future of the organization is described in as full terms as possible.

Day three of the consolidation conference is set aside for tidying up loose ends, dealing with any concerns and for preparing a scorecard (goals, measures, timeframes) and an implementation plan. It is also a time of celebration – the past, the present and the future. The two evenings of the conference were free and allowed for some wonderful self-organizing social and community-building activity.

As we entered the final day tired, with more hard work ahead, we planned and agreed on a steering team to oversee the implementation tasks. There was a great sense of history, achievement, and celebration. Our work had been undertaken seriously. A vision for the future of the YMCA had emerged through the past and through the current context of national turmoil and violence.

What has it all Meant?

From my perspective as an external facilitator, it has been an experience full of excitement and learning. Seeing search conferences conducted in Arabic – not understanding the content, but fully appreciating the process – the moods, the energy, the flow, were very rewarding. The coming together of all the threads, sometimes rather messy ones, at the consolidation conference was a very emotional experience for me and for many of the participants.

For the YMCA in Jerusalem and Palestine it meant:

♦ a new direction and set of priorities – openly, participatively created and shared by all
♦ a significant experience of being involved together across all sections and levels of the organization. A deep and meaningful community-building experience
♦ a new ethos of openness and participation

♦ a greater sense of belief and trust in each other, especially across programs and levels
♦ a challenging period of implementing our vision and plan
♦ a reaffirmation of the mission of the YMCA to future generations of Palestinian young people
♦ hope in the future

The Road Continues

Implementation steps are underway. Reports and reporting processes have diffused the outputs of the consolidation conference to all organizational members and to external stakeholders.

But there have been and continue to be significant obstacles. The levels of violence and confrontation have escalated in the period from December 2001 to March 2002. Because of the closures and blockades, inter-YMCA meetings are often impossible. The economic consequences have resulted in the closure of the East Jerusalem YMCA hostel, with an obvious impact on staff.

An important six-month review and follow up to the consolidation conference (a full re-gathering of all the participants) had to be delayed because of the prevailing circumstances. Levels of human and organizational tolerance are tested to the extreme, no less the RRE process. Small groups meet and work where they can. The YMCA leadership attempts to find creative and adaptive approaches to implementing and building the "new future" with their people.

In Conclusion

The RRE process has been a journey that has released much human energy. A new ethos, culture, and approach to leadership are emerging. There can be no turning back.

RGA salutes the leaders and staff of the YMCA for their courageous endeavors and their commitment to the future. Many members of the board, of management, and of the staff could be singled out, not least the internal facilitators.

May future generations of Palestinian young people come to realize their dreams through your courageous searching through the past, the present, and into the future, as you continue to build the Palestinian YMCA.

Reference
[1] RGA Consulting – Renewal, Growth, and Alignment of Organizations Through their People.

Chapter 13
The Future of
the YMCA of
Palestine

Epilogue: The Future of Search

As we have seen throughout *Futures That Work*, search conferences produce people dedicated to making their desirable future happen. Not only do people walk away committed to their plan, they also learn how to search so they can continue to adapt and change their plan as they go forward. After the search, people go back to their organization or community and spread their energy and excitement about what they experienced and the plan they developed. In this way, the search community spreads to others as the number of people involved in the plan grows with time. That's what a search conference does. It makes it possible for people to enact futures they will make happen in the world – systems that become adaptive and successful in ever-changing environments.

The world is getting more and more turbulent and uncertain in the 21st century. We face worldwide terrorism with its continuous threats of violence, the unknown impact of globalization, the increasing effects of environmental deterioration, and the continuing gap between rich and poor. Some say changes are happening so fast now and have become such a permanent feature that we are moving into a period of super-turbulence. Instead of the using the metaphor of a turbulent sky, the newly emerging image of change is the vortex – a whirlpool spinning out of control.[1]

The super-turbulent environment that is developing before our eyes has several effects on any system within it. A system – whether organization or community – can fail to adapt in this super-turbulent environment, becoming rigid and inflexible. Instead of learning from its environment, it can become dogmatic, shutting down the learning process, not letting in outside information. Inside these systems, people and groups become polarized, working at cross-purposes with one another. Failing to learn and cooperate together, these systems can reach stalemate, unable to plan for or shape their own futures in the world.

While super-turbulence isn't happening everywhere all the time, examples of systems experiencing the effects of super-turbulence abound in the world.[2] The Middle East continues to be stuck in a quagmire of turmoil. Africa and other parts of the developing world cannot find a way out of poverty and health problems and threats such as the AIDS epidemic. Big cities around the world experience unrelenting crime, pollution, and poverty. Meanwhile, the international rate of species extinction escalates all the time.

Companies and organizations of all types face super-turbulence as their business environments heat up with predatory competition. Corporations are responding with increasing bankruptcies, buy-outs, and employee downsizing – anything to survive. Other companies engage in desperate and questionable financial schemes. And labor management disputes polarize many companies, causing an impasse, while others have problems bringing products to market due to strategic gridlock. The way out of this mess is for us to revitalize our companies, communities, and organizations through cooperative, purposeful action towards our most desirable futures.

Hope lives in the stories in this book about how brave people are standing up to big problems in Croatia and Palestine. The Nebraska Department of Public Institutions fights off the bureaucratic inattention to mental health problems by bringing together people from different parts of the system to address the problem together. A community in suburban Denver tackles juvenile crime by putting judge, police, teacher, and juvenile offender at the same table to unleash their creative energy. Water engineers cross their conflicted boundaries to develop a cooperative water plan for a region.

A Hewlett Packard plant faces up to its failing business strategy by having managers jointly decide which products to keep making and which to drop. A small salon transforms its business into a spa with the help of employees. A Microsoft product group transcends polarization with a new strategy and organization. The South African Department of Water Affairs and Forestry engages stakeholders throughout the country in breaking through the problem of supplying everyone with drinkable water.

All these stories have some things in common. The people in these stories faced big problems, many of which seemed insurmountable at the time. They crossed traditional boundaries to bring together people from all parts of the system – management and workers, engineers from cities in conflict, citizens and leaders, police and offenders. These people cooperated to create solutions and committed to specific actions to make their future work. And they used search conferences to do it.

We started *Futures That Work* by saying that now is the time for search conferencing to take off and become an even more widespread way of bringing about change in communities and organizations. The reason is that today's fast-changing world requires creative, cooperative methods for engaging people in revitalizing their institutions. We encourage you to follow the path of change that the courageous leaders, managers, citizens, and consultants embarked upon, whose stories are told in this book. Be creative like several contributors to this book, who, guided by search conference principles, modified the basic search conference design and developed new ways to do participative planning, engaging large numbers of people in discovering their desirable futures together.

In *Futures That Work*, we have provided you with all the basics for using a search conference. You should now have a good sense of the basic design of a typical search conference, with a detailed example from the Nebraska mental health system. You have learned about the principles underlying every search conference. You have an understanding of how to effectively prepare and follow up a search. And you have an array of stories describing how search conferences were done in a wide variety of systems including communities, companies, and all kinds of organizations. We hope you will use the search conference to revitalize your organization or community and find futures that work for you.

References

1   Baburoglu, Oguz. "The Vortical Environment: The Fifth in the Emery-Trist Levels of Organizational Environments," in Trist, Eric et al. (eds.) *The Social Engagement of Social Science: A Tavistock Anthology, Volume III: The Socio-Ecological Perspective*, Philadelphia: University of Pennsylvania Press, 1997.

2   Wright, Susan & Morley, David (eds.) *Learning Works: Searching for Organizational Futures: A Tribute to Eric Trist.* Toronto: The ABL Group, 1989.

Bibliography

Asch, S. *Social Psychology*. Englewood Cliffs, N.J.: Prentice-Hall, 1952.

Bion, W. R. *Experiences in Groups*. New York: Basic Books, 1959.

Emery, M. (ed.) *Participative Design for Participative Democracy*. Canberra, Australia. Australian National University, 1993.

Emery, M. "Organizing for the Successful Implementation of Planning: The Two Stage Model of Active Adaptation", unpublished paper, 1996.

Emery, M. "Search Conferences: State of the Art", unpublished paper, 1994.

Emery, M. & Purser, R. *The Search Conference: A Powerful Method for Planning Organizational Change and Community Action*. San Francisco: Jossey-Bass, 1996.

Hoffman, Chris. *The Hoop and the Tree: A Compass for Finding a Deeper Relationship with All Life*. San Francisco: Council Oaks Books, 2000.

Rehm, Robert. *People in Charge: Creating Self-Managing Workplaces*. Stroud, UK: Hawthorn Press, 1999.

Rogers, Everett M. *Diffusion of Innovations*. New York: The Free Press, 1995.

Trist, Eric, Emery, Fred & Murray, Hugh. *The Social Engagement of Social Science: A Tavistock Anthology, Volume*

III: The Socio-Ecological Perspective. Philadelphia: University of Pennsylvania Press, 1997.

Weisbord, Marvin R. *Discovering Common Ground*. San Francisco: Berrett-Koehler, 1992.

Weisbord, M. and Janoff, S. *Future Search: An Action Guide to finding Common Ground in Organizations and Communities*. San Francisco: Berret-Kohler, 1995.

Wright, S. & Morley, D. (eds.) *Learning Works: Searching for Organizational Futures*. Toronto: ABL Publications, 1989.

Resources

Tom Devane
tdevane@tomdevane.com
Web site: tomdevane.com
Telephone: 303 898 6172

Robert Rehm and Nancy Cebula
People in Charge
1460 Judson Drive
Boulder, Colorado USA 80303

Telephone: 303 499 1607
Fax: 303 494 2337
Web site: www.peopleincharge.org
E-mail: bob@peopleincharge.org
         nancy@peopleincharge.org

Fran Ryan

Fran works with large and small groups in organizations and communities to help them clarify their priorities for the future and then get organized to make it happen. Current work includes projects in public sector reform, manufacturing, sport and community development, and sustainable agriculture, all in the UK.

Contact Fran at:
People in Charge Ltd
Telephone: t +44 (0) 1865 396592
           m +44 (0) 7889 209448
E-mail: fran@peopleincharge.co.uk
        fran@voicematters.org

Martin Large

Martin Large works with People in Charge, VoiceMatters and as an independent facilitator. His recent work draws on conflict transformation, participative strategic planning using search, participative design, mentoring and action learning. Current work focuses on using search to develop a performing arts center, a new sixth form college, a social enterprise center and for developing community land trusts.

Contact Martin at:
Hawthorn House
1 Lansdown Lane
Stroud
Gloucestershire GL5 1BJ

Telephone: +44 1453 757040
Fax: +44 1453 751138
E-mail: mhclarge@aol.com
        martin@voicematters.org

Graham Benjamin

Graham Benjamin is an independent consultant in organizational change, practicing worldwide on whole system change and major project alignment.

Contact Graham at:
E-mail: graham.benjamin@btinternet
Phone in the UK: +44 1908 261260

Catherine Bradshaw and Joan Roberts

Catherine Bradshaw and Joan Roberts work together in an alliance called Open Systems Design Associates (OSDA). OSDA helps organizations thrive in today's turbulent environment by drawing powerfully from the talent, knowledge and creativity of their people. Catherine and Joan use methods such as the search conference that engage people in the ongoing creation of their workplace.

Catherine Bradshaw, MA, Whole Systems Design
Contact Catherine at:
Open System Design Associates
216 Gainsborough Rd.
Toronto, Ontario, M4L 3C6

Telephone: 416 406 4232
Fax: 416 406 0868
E-mail: cbradshaw@common-ground.com

Joan Roberts, MA, Human Systems Intervention
Contact Joan at:
Open System Design Associates
390 Harvie Ave
Toronto, Ontario M6E 4L8

Telephone/Fax: 416 651 2719
E-mail: joanroberts@sympatico.ca

Evangeline Caridas

Evangeline Caridas helps organizations achieve results through unleashing the creative power of their people, with over fourteen years management and consulting experience. She published the groundbreaking results from her study, "Flow and Optimal Performance in the Workplace," in *Rediscovering the Soul of Business.*

Contact Evangeline at:
Caridas Consulting Group
3223 Albans Rd.
Houston, Texas 77005

Telephone: 713 629 5692
Fax: 713 629 5697
E-mail: ecaridas@flowmanagement.net
Website: www.flowmanagement.net

Frank Heckman

Frank Heckman runs a consultancy/practicum for empowerment, organizational renewal, and social innovation: Connecting people, organizations, and environment. He has managed in the course of the last ten years many search conferences for clients varying from government, production plants, hi-tech companies, school systems, "main streets," communities and neighborhoods.

Contact Frank at:
Spirit in Action
Lange Nieustraat 55 bis
3512 PD Utrecht
The Netherlands

Telephone: (31) 030 2304875
Fax: (31) 030 2304928
E-mail: frankheckman@freeler.nl

Steve Hobbs

Steve Hobbs is a director of RGA Consulting. Via RGA he is committed to making a positive contribution to the process of transformation in the new democratic South Africa.

Contact Steve at:
E-mail: hobbs@ionet.co.za
Mobile phone: (0027) 82 558 3070

RGA Consulting (Renewal, Growth, and Alignment of organizations through their people) focuses on the design and facilitation of large-scale, whole-system strategies for organizational renewal and alignment. Work is split among the private, public, and NGO sectors in such places as South Africa, Lesotho, Australia, England, Ethiopia, Sri Lanka, Switzerland, and Palestine

53 Peace Road, Kloof, 3610, South Africa
Tel/Fax: 0027 (31) 764 6256
Website: www.RGAconsulting.com

Dennis Mayhew

Dennis Mayhew is an organization development consultant living in Chicago. He focuses his work on large-scale redesign, change management, strategic planning, and leadership and team development.

Contact Dennis at:
E-mail: dennismayhew@msn.com

Pete Peschang
Pete Peschang has an extensive background providing social services to Alaska native tribes and has incorporated large-group process work to promote healing and community development in rural villages.

Contact Pete at:
Future Focus Consulting
HC 60 Box 282
Copper Center, Alaska 99573
Telephone: 907 822 5471
Fax: 907 822 5472
E-mail: pgpeschang@netscape.net

Other Books from Hawthorn Press

People in Charge
Creating self managing
workplaces
Robert Rehm

A step-by-step guide to
designing self managing
workplaces. Powerful and
practical, Participative Design
enables companies to create
more productive workplaces
and better results. Here are
the tools for creating self
managing workplaces using
Participative Design. The concepts, do-it-yourself guide and
helpful examples show how people can re-design their work.
The result is a more productive workplace full of energy,
learning, quality and pride. And people in charge of their work.

288pp; 243 x 189mm; paperback; 1 869 890 87 6

*'Frankly, I find most books on this subject useless. This one is
different. It is filled with practical theories, and business related
examples, that I can use on a daily basis.'*
Kevin Purcell, Director of Organization Consulting,
Microsoft Corporation

Confronting Conflict
A first-aid kit for handling conflict
Friedrich Glasl

Conflict costs! When tensions and differences are ignored they grow into conflicts, injuring relationships, groups and organisations. So, how can we tackle conflict successfully?

Confronting Conflict is authoritative and up to date, containing new examples, exercises theory and techniques. You can start by assessing the symptoms and causes of conflict, and ask, 'Am I fanning the flames?' And then consider, 'How can I behave constructively rather than attack or avoid others?'

Here are tools to; Analyse symptoms, types, causes of conflict, hot or cold, personal chemistry, structures or environment; understand how temperaments affect conflicts; acknowledge when you have a conflict, understand conflict escalation, how to lessen conflict through changing behaviour, attitudes and perceptions; practise developing considerate confrontation, seizing golden moments, and strengthening empathy.

Confronting Conflict will be useful for managers, facilitators, management lecturers and professionals such as teachers and community workers, mediators and workers in dispute resolution.

Dr Friedrich Glasl has worked with conflict resolution in companies, schools and communities for over 30 years, earning him and his techniques enormous respect. He has written many books, including *Enterprise of the Future*.

192pp; 216 x 138mm; paperback; 1 869 890 71 X

Navigator
Men's Development Workbook
James Traeger, Jenny Daisley and Liz Willis

Navigator is one of the very first personal and professional development workbooks in the UK specifically developed for all men at work, on their own or in relationships and as fathers and sons. Life for men is changing, and changing fast. Many men are asking who they are and where they, and their expectations of life, fit in with these rapid changes. Navigator provides individual men with a down-to-earth way of tackling many of these issues.

Navigator forms the basis of a 3 month Men's Development Programme recently researched and piloted inside a wide range of UK organisations, including BT Mobile, Braintree District Council, Midland Bank, NatWest UK, Wolverhampton MBC, The University of Cambridge and The University of London.

Navigator is full of positive thinking and good humour and is packed with ideas, examples and practical exercises with the points illustrated with cartoons and real case studies. Contents include; realistic self-assessment; challenging expectations; a man's world, clarifying values; taking risks and making changes; physical and feelings fitness; setting a goal strategy that works; assertiveness for men; putting yourself across.

288pp; 297 x 210mm; paperback; 1 869 890 80 9

Springboard
Women's Development Workbook
Liz Willis and Jenny Daisley
Illustrated by Viv Quillin

Springboard helps you do what you want to do in your life and work. It gives you the ideas and skills to take more control of your life and then gives you the boost in self confidence to start making things happen. *Springboard* is for all women at work; whether you are in full time or part time employment, considering employment, wanting to return to work, just starting out, or approaching retirement – *Springboard* helps you to be the best you can be!

Springboard is a workbook packed with ideas, exercises and examples that you can either work through on your own, or with two or three others. It is down-to-earth, practical and full of positive thinking and good humour, with the points illustrated with cartoons and real case studies. You can work through the workbook on its own or as part of the Springboard Women's Development Programme. Contents include; assertiveness; setting goals; what you've got going for you; finding support; the world about you; blowing your own trumpet; more energy – less anxiety; making things happen; your personal resource bank; balancing home and work; networking; useful addresses.

5th edition; fully revised and updated
320pp; 297 x 210mm; illustrations; cartoons; paperback; 1 869 890 10 8

'Inspir-actical *is how I would describe* Springboard. *It inspires women to decide what they most want to achieve and then, very practically, helps them do it. It's fun and involving.*'
Valerie Hammond, Chief Executive Officer, Roffey Park
Management Institute

Springing Forward
Gina Harris and Liza Edwards

If you could have anything, what would it be? Are you making the most of your potential? Have you ever felt that there was something you are supposed to achieve, but can't seem to start?

Don't just dream about it – make it happen!

Welcome to the essential handbook for all women wanting to make the most of who they are. *Springing Forward* is packed full of practical steps, sound advice and inspiration to support you – whatever your goal, whatever your situation. Each stage is also supported by quotes and stories from women around the world, drawing on the global success of the Springboard Women's Development Programme, and celebrating women's achievements.

Springing Forward shows how women can make genuine, positive changes to their everyday lives. Most importantly, the writers realise that you do have priorities other than nurturing yourself, and they tackle the path ahead with practical realistic advice, frankness and a good dose of humour.

Topics covered include; bringing the ideal into the real; healthy selfishness; getting organised, – space, finances and time; the internet and how you can benefit/the internet for real people; values, priorities and acting on decisions; genuine communication; simplicity, serenity and the future … and enjoying it all!

128pp; 210 x 148mm; cartoons; 1 869 890 40 X

Workways: Seven Stars to Steer By

Biography Workbook for Building
a More Enterprising Life
*Kees Locher and Jos van
der Brug*

This biography workbook helps
you consider your working life,
and make more conscious
choices, at a time of great change
in our 'workways'. Background
readings, thirty seven exercises
and creative activities are carefully structured for individuals
or self-help groups.

352pp; 297 x 210mm; paperback;
1 869 890 89 2

The Enterprise of the Future

Moral Intuition in Leadership and
Organisational Development
Friedrich Glasl

Friedrich Glasl looks at the future role
of the organisation in the community,
and the opportunity it offers for
personal development. He addresses the
need to expand consciousness beyond
the organisation to the 'shared destiny'
it holds with the community and with
whom it shares a common enterprise.

160pp; 216 x 138mm; paperback; 1 869 890 79 5

Manhood
An action plan for changing men's lives
Steve Biddulph

'Most men don't have a life.' So begins the most powerful, practical and honest book ever to be written about men and boys. Not about our problems – but about how we can find the joy and energy of being in a male body with a man's mind and spirit – about men's liberation.

Steve Biddulph, author of *Raising Boys* and the million-seller *The Secret of Happy Children*, writes about the turning point that men have reached – as reflected in films like *The Full Monty*. He gives practical personal answers to how things can be different from the bedroom to the workplace. He tells powerful stories about healing the rift between fathers and sons. About friendship. How women and men can get along in dynamic harmonious ways. How boys can be raised to be healthy men.

Manhood has had a profound emotional impact on tens of thousands of readers worldwide, and has been passed from son to father, friend to friend, husband to wife, with the simple message 'you must read this!'

'Steve Biddulph should be in the UK what he is in Australia, the household name in the business of raising boys and being a man.'
Dorothy Rowe, psychologist and writer

272pp; 216 x 138mm; 12 black and white photographs; paperback;
1 869 890 99 X

Soul Weaving
How to shape your destiny and inspire your dreams
Betty Staley

Soul Weaving is an invitation to weave a design for the Soul's journey bringing together the colours and textures of our personality to reveal pattern and meaning. *Soul Weaving* is the most comprehensive introduction to the temperaments, archetypes and soul qualities, as defined by Rudolf Steiner, which enable us to better understand ourselves and our relationship to the world.

This book shows us how to; transform our temperament; realise and integrate our soul type; understand the influences of the archetypal points of view; make life changes such as choosing a spiritual path, living in balance, cultivating the power of love, and much more.

Betty Staley's interest in psychology started at graduate school in the 1950's and has never left her. She has taught for over 30 years in Steiner Waldorf schools and lectures at Rudolf Steiner College, Sacramento. A companion to *Tapestries, Soul Weaving* is a lively and authoritative introduction to spiritual psychology. Betty is also the author of the best seller *Between Form and Freedom – a practical guide to the teenage years*, which has been translated into Dutch, German and Japanese.

Soul Weaving will interest counsellors, teachers, educators, doctors, humanistic and transpersonal students and facilitators.

240pp; 216 x 138mm; paperback; 1 869 890 05 1

Tapestries
Weaving Life's Journey
Betty Staley

Tapestries gives a moving and wise guide to women's life phases. Drawing on original biographies of a wide variety of women, informed by personal experience and by her understanding of anthroposophy, Betty Staley offers a vivid account of life journeys. This book helps readers reflect on their own lives and prepare for the next step in weaving their own biographical tapestry.

336pp; 216 x 138mm; paperback; 1 869 890 15 9

Money for a Better World
Rudolf Mees

This slim volume re-works our attitudes towards handling money and presents finance on a human scale. It discusses alternative ways of looking at money in our modern world and realistic methods of approaching borrowing, saving and lending.

64pp; 216 x 138mm; paperback; 1 869 890 26 4

Vision in Action
Working with Soul and Spirit in Small Organisations
Christopher Schaefer, Tÿno Voors

Vision in Action is a workbook for those involved in social creation – in collaborative deeds that can influence the social environment in which we live and where our ideas and actions can matter. This is a user-friendly, hands-on guide for developing healthy small organisations – organisations with soul and spirit.

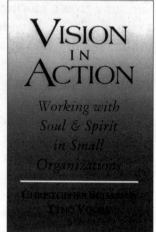

Chapters include:
Starting Initiatives;
Getting Going;
Ways of Working Together;
Funding Initiatives;
Vision, Mission, and Long-Range Planning;
Fund-raising.

'*Many readers will find* Vision *a valuable source of inspiration and help.*'
James Robertson

'*Socially-oriented initiatives and small organizations play a vital role in a healthy, evolving society.* Vision in Action *offers important and practical perspectives that capture this essence.*'
Will Brinton, President of Woods End Laboratory

256pp; 235 x 152mm; paperback; 1 869 890 88 4

Ken Sprague: People's Artist
John Green

Ken Sprague is a print-maker, posterman, painter, cartoonist, muralist, banner maker, psycho-drama tutor and art teacher. He is a legendary storyteller, with moving and amusing stories to enliven his pictures. Twice winner of the National Council for Industrial Design's poster of the year award, he has frequently exhibited. Uniquely, he is probably the only British artist with a life long connection with the trade union movement. His BBC Omnibus film, The Posterman, was very popular.

Full of good stories, this biography offers fascinating insights into the crisis of art. It asks how art can be reclaimed for ordinary people and communities. Ken Sprague is an artist who, as a radical freethinker, does not fit easily into any category. He invites us to take creative action for a better, more beautiful world.

John Green is a journalist, film maker, artist and trade union official, with a life-long interest in art.

'This celebration of Ken Sprague's life is to be welcomed; he, as much as anyone, deserves it.' Tony Benn

'This book reflects the varied life and interests of a splendid character, racy, determined, invariably smiling with people and at life.' Jack Jones, former General Secretary, TGWU

160pp, including 16pp colour section; 275 x 215mm; paperback;
1 903458 34 X

Orders

If you have difficulties ordering Hawthorn Press books from a bookshop, you can order direct from:

Booksource
32 Finlas Street, Glasgow, G22 5DU
Tel: +(44) (0) 141 558 1366
Fax: +(44) (0) 141 557 0189
E-mail: orders@booksource.net
Website: **www.booksource.net**

Please note that *People in Charge* and *Futures that Work* are available in North America from:

New Society Publishers,
Consortium, 1045 Westgate Drive #90,
Saint Paul MN 55114-1065.
Tel: +(1) 800 283 3572

Further information / Book catalogue

Hawthorn Press
1 Lansdown Lane, Stroud
Gloucestershire, GL5 1BJ, UK
Tel: +(44) (0) 1453 757040
Fax: +(44) (0) 1453 751138
E-mail: info@hawthornpress.com
Website: **www.hawthornpress.com**

Books can be ordered direct from the Hawthorn Press website.

Dear Reader

If you wish to follow up your reading of this book, please tick the boxes below as appropriate, fill in your name and address and return to Hawthorn Press:

☐ Please send me a catalogue of other Hawthorn Press books.

☐ Please send me details of Personal Development events and courses.

My feedback about Personal Development:

Name ————————————————————————————

Address ————————————————————————————

————————————————————————————————

————————————————————————————————

Postcode ——————————————— Tel no ———————————

Please return to:
Hawthorn Press, Hawthorn House, 1 Lansdown Lane, Stroud,
Glos. GL5 1BJ, UK

or Fax (01453) 751138

FTW